MANAGING ACQUISITIONS AND VENDOR RELATIONS

A How-To-Do-It Manual

HEATHER S. MILLER

HOW-TO-DO-IT MANUALS FOR LIBRARIES

Number 23

NEAL-SCHUMAN PUBLISHERS, INC.
New York, London

Published by Neal-Schuman Publishers, Inc.
100 Varick Street
New York, NY 10013

Copyright © 1992 by Heather S. Miller

All rights reserved. Reproduction of this book, in whole or in
part, without written permission of the publisher is prohibited.

Text in Chapter 6 is based on an article reprinted with permission from *Library
Acquisitions: Practice & Theory,* Vol. 14, by Heather S. Miller: "How Not To Buy Books
for Libraries: Contracts, Bids, and Recent Developments in New York State," copyright
1990 by Pergamon Press Ltd.

Printed and bound in the United States of America

Library of Congress Cataloging-in-Publication Data

Miller, Heather Swan.
    Managing acquisitions and vendor relations : a how-to-do-it manual
/ Heather S. Miller.
      p. cm. — (How-to-do-it manuals for libraries ; no. 23)
    Includes bibliographical references and index.
    ISBN 1-55570-111-6
    1. Acquisitions (Libraries)—Handbooks, manuals, etc.
2. Libraries and booksellers—Handbooks, manuals, etc.   I. Title.
II. Series.
Z689.M48 1992
025.2—dc20   92-19828
                                                                     CIP

CONTENTS

	Preface	vii
	Acknowledgments	ix
1	Some Basics	3
	The Acquisitions Department	3
	Collection Development Policy	4
	The Vendors	5
	The Partnership	8
2	What Lies Ahead?	11
	Technical Standards	11
	Full Text Online	15
3	Choosing Book Vendors	19
	Vendor or publisher?	19
	Discounts and Cost-Plus Pricing	21
	Value-Added Services	23
	Price vs. Service	24
	Making the Choice	24
4	Choosing Serials Vendors	31
	Periodicals	31
	Continuations	46
	Making the Choice	48
5	Becoming Partners	51
	Orders	51
	The Third Partner	52
	Rush Orders	53
	Reports	53
	Claims	54
	Returns	55

	Cancellations	56
	Errors	56
	Payment	57
	Invoices	58
	Communication	58
	Automation	59
6	**Contracts and Bidding**	**61**
	The Book Contract	61
	Bidding	62
	Vendor Opinion	64
	What Can Be Done?	65
7	**Approval Plans**	**69**
	Origins	69
	Approval Plans Today	70
	Management Considerations	70
	Discount	73
	View from the Vendor's Side	73
	Profiles	74
	Management Reports	74
	Is an Approval Plan Desirable?	75
	Choosing a Plan	75
	A Special Partnership	76
	Automation	78
	A Futuristic View	79
8	**Out of the Main Stream**	**83**
	Nonprint Media	83
	CD-ROM	86
	Government Publications	88
	The Partnership	89

9	Out-of-Print	93
	Librarians vs. Book Dealers	94
	A Whole New World	94
	Out-of-Print Status	95
	Organizing OP Purchasing	96
	Understanding the Business	98
	Matching Needs to Available Titles	100
	Which Dealer and How Many?	101
	Back Issues of Serials	103
	Online Matching Services	104
10	The Pricing Problem	107
	Prices	107
	Proliferation of Information	111
	Inflation	113
	Weak Dollar	113
	Library Budgets	114
	The Pricing Battlefront	115
	One World	116
	Where Do We Go From Here?	117
	The Partnership	122
11	Evaluation	125
	A Professional Responsibility	125
	Taking the Vendor's Measure	126
	Methodologies	126
	Library Preparation	129
	Libraries' Impact on Vendor Performance	130
	Evaluation Approaches	131
	What Vendors Think	135
	Evaluative Studies	136
	Evaluating the Library	138

		The Partnership	139
		Communication	140
12		A Question of Ethics	141
		Ethics and the Vendor	142
		Ethics and the Librarian	143
		The Bottom Line	149
Appendix A		Tracking Library Materials Prices	151
Appendix B		Keeping Up With Vendor-Related Issues	155
Appendix C		What Librarians Think of Vendors	159
		Bibliography	167
		Index	189

PREFACE

Obtaining materials for library collections is the raison d'etre of the acquisitions department whether it consists of one person or many. Generally, the acquisitions librarian purchases these materials from a vendor—a wholesaler. And, all too often, acquisitions librarians educate themselves on the job, through trial and error, having received little practical training in library school. *Managing Acquisitions and Vendor Relations* is intended to help acquisitions librarians learn from the experiences of others in the all-important area of dealing with those vendors who provide books to libraries. It is at once a guide to developing fruitful partnerships and a point of departure for the expansion of the unique librarian-vendor relationship in the future.

Material for this book has come from many sources, and it is intended to be used in many types of libraries. While my own experiences in a moderately large academic library have colored my outlook, I believe that outlook is broad enough for wide application. It is recommended that this book be used in conjunction with other writings on the organization and management of acquisitions operations and the purchasing of library materials. Particularly useful are *Buying Books* and *Buying Serials* cited in the bibliographies for Chapters 3 and 4, respectively.

Assisted to a large extent by automation, vendors now offer services far beyond the mere provision of books. Use of vendors' databases and vendor-supplied data can significantly augment a library's store of information.

The huge databases developed by subscription agents and made available to the library community are noteworthy examples of the blending of library- and vendor-supplied information sources. It is also an indication of the complex situation facing acquisitions librarians who must evaluate and choose among such services.

With library users demanding more and more information, publishers providing it in an array of formats, and vendors vying for library orders (all in a time of reduced purchasing power), acquisitions librarians must be knowledgeable, evaluative, and assertive in dealing with vendors. By viewing vendors as partners in the provision of information and by making informed and sometimes difficult decisions regarding them and their services, librarians will benefit not only their library but, more importantly, their clientele.

ACKNOWLEDGMENTS

It is no easy task to give thanks where thanks is due, especially when inspiration, insight, guidance, information, and encouragement have been provided over a period of years. The comments, opinions, and even complaints of vendors, librarians, and co-workers have made their way onto these pages. To all of these individuals, I am most grateful.

Other works, cited in the bibliography, have been influential as well as inspiring. Participants in recent Charleston Conferences receive special thanks. This forum for the exchange of ideas among librarians and vendors is unique and never fails to provide thought-provoking material for us all. Many issues discussed at these conferences have made their way into these pages.

Participants at the 1990 conference and readers of *Against the Grain*, the newsletter that grew out of the Charleston Conference, responded generously to my call for input. All of their comments have been incorporated into *Managing Acquisitions and Vendor Relations* in one way or another.

In addition, my special thanks go to Sharon Bonk, Assistant Director for User Services, University Libraries, University at Albany, who has prodded and cajoled me repeatedly over the years, who first nudged me into acquisitions work, and who continues to provide assistance and inspiration. I am grateful to Gillian McCombs, Assistant Director for Technical Services and Systems, University at Albany, for her unflagging support, for approving my sabbatical request during an extremely difficult fiscal year, and for being willing to check in periodicals and delve ever more deeply into acquisitions while I was writing. Meredith Butler, Director of Libraries, University at Albany, who also supported my sabbatical and has long been a champion of librarians' participation in the larger academic world, is gratefully acknowledged.

A number of vendors were remarkably generous, willingly sharing their expertise with me. Richard Abel, to whom most of us on both sides of the librarian/vendor equation owe more than we realize, spoke at length with me about his vision of the librarian/vendor relationship. Celia Scher Wagner shared with me some of her insights on ethics and evaluation. Jonathan Waring shared his views of the business of providing materials to libraries. Elliot Ephraim allowed me to interrupt his work and explained at length the business of supplying out-of-print books to libraries, despite the fact that the University at Albany must surely be one of his worst customers. I cannot thank these colleagues enough.

Special thanks go to those who tolerantly read the manuscript in one or more of its nascent stages. To Jane Maddox and Barry Fast, who have shared their considerable knowledge with me in recent years, and especially to Barry, who also read the manuscript and carefully, thoughtfully commented on it, I am very much in debt.

I must also acknowledge the experience I have received at the University at Albany and the people in and beyond the University Libraries with whom I have been associated. In a challenging environment in which to mold a vision of acquisitions, many partnerships have been formed from which I have benefited greatly. Together we have accomplished a great deal. My own staff in Acquisitions deserves more reward than I can provide. They have worked hard and with good humor while I was on sabbatical, through staff shortages and spending freezes, amid increasing expectations. No mention of the department would be complete without expressing my thanks to Suzanne Irving, who managed the department in my absence.

Many thanks go, too, to my husband Norton and my son Andrew for their forbearance, cooperation, and advice during this year.

Last but not least by any means, my sincere thanks to Cathie Gifford of Key Information Processing, who reworked an inexpertly typed manuscript and made it publisher friendly.

The single greatest service your vendor can provide you is to remain profitable.

Ed Lochman
"Truth in Vending"
Panel Presentation, Charleston Conference, 1984

1 SOME BASICS

THE ACQUISITIONS DEPARTMENT:

ITS MISSION AND THE ROLE OF THE ACQUISITIONS LIBRARIAN

The acquisitions librarian plays a crucial role in the provision of library services, a role demanding a sophisticated level of knowledge and skill. The acquisitions department, even if consisting of only one person, is the filter through which every item destined for the library's collection must pass. Whether selection is done in the acquisitions department or elsewhere, the actual ordering, receiving, and approving of invoices occurs in acquisitions. In some libraries, a separate serials department performs some of these functions either independently or in conjunction with the acquisitions department. Regardless of departmental names or specifics of organization, acquisitions functions are recognizable and discrete, and it is to those functions that this book refers when using the term "acquisitions department." It is often the acquisitions department that has the last opportunity to prevent duplication, to identify potential conflicts with existing approval plans and standing orders, and to recognize spurious entries—not to mention plain, old-fashioned typographical errors.

The matching of orders to vendors is a delicate business requiring good judgment and knowledge of past experience with a variety of vendors. Personal contact between librarian and vendor is essential for the librarian to keep informed about a vendor's services and pricing policies. Once orders have been placed, claim cycles and vendor reports must be incorporated into the process of monitoring the status of each order. When books arrive, they must be checked against order records. Errors must be dealt with, receiving procedures followed, and the books sent on to the next step, which is often the cataloging department. Invoices must be verified and processed for payment, frequently in accord with complex institutional requirements. All of this must be done in the most efficient and orderly manner possible, not only to facilitate the receipt of material, but also to permit its retrieval from the work flow once it has arrived in the library and to hasten payment to the vendor.

Beyond this, it is in the acquisitions department that knowledge of the publishing industry, vendors' services and shortcomings, currency fluctuations, accounting practices, and institutional purchasing requirements are concentrated. Management skills necessary to organize and direct the varied aspects of the acquisition of library materials, awareness of legal and ethical issues, and accountability for the entire complex of operations must rest with those responsible for these departments: the acquisitions librarians.

All acquisitions librarians operate under the same mandate, whether stated or implied: to obtain the materials their libraries need at the best price with the best service. This is a responsibility requiring knowledge of publishers and vendors; developments in the publishing industry; condition of the dollar and, often, foreign money markets; knowledge of one's own institution's funds, requirements, and restrictions, which can be formidable; plus organizational and managerial abilities essential for maintaining the orderly functioning of the department. Communication skills are essential because acquisitions librarians must be prepared to explain the status of orders to co-workers and patrons, while communicating to vendors both pleasure and displeasure with their performance. It may also be necessary to conduct training sessions for staff members in other departments on how to determine whether a book has been ordered, possibly including the use of an automated system. Elements of business, personnel management, teaching, and diplomacy are all incorporated into the acquisitions librarian's role.

COLLECTION DEVELOPMENT POLICY

A detailed, written collection development policy is essential for unifying the library's approach to acquiring material. Particularly in lean financial situations, libraries need to know what their goals are so that their precious resources can be most effectively expended. The process of preparing a collection development policy forces the library to clarify its overall goals and to define clearly what it can and cannot acquire and house. This document becomes the foundation on which selection decisions are based. It can be a basis for discussion with patrons, sales representatives, faculty members, administrators, and others regarding what will be purchased.

This is not to say that the policy can never be changed. In fact, it should be reviewed regularly and updated as needed. This only makes it a stronger, more useful document because it will always be up to date, reflecting current realities.

THE VENDORS

WHO THEY ARE, WHAT THEY DO, WHY WE USE THEM

Those who supply materials to the library are the other half of the equation; without a source of supply no material would ever reach the library's shelves. Library materials may come from donors, through exchange agreements, or by purchase from publishers, individuals, or intermediaries referred to as vendors who obtain materials from publishers and provide them to libraries.

Businesses that specialize in supplying libraries with books and periodicals do not have a long history in this country, dating back only to the 1930s and burgeoning after World War II. Libraries formerly purchased books directly from publishers or from retail booksellers. However, given the multitude of books published today, the large number of publishers, the volatility of the publishing industry, and the disorderly state of book distribution in the United States, it is difficult to imagine libraries doing so today.

With over 800,000 titles in *Books In Print* alone, library suppliers provide an essential service in distributing publishers' material and providing support services. Vendors impose at least a modicum of order on the distribution end of an industry that, in North America at least, is ever changing and proliferating. The vendor serves as a "translator" of sorts between publishers and libraries.

Some publishers refuse to deal with intermediaries, demanding that all books be purchased directly from them. This increases the library's paperwork and record keeping and, often, its problems and correspondence as well. Many book dealers specialize in service to libraries, although some also sell to bookstores. Some specialize in certain subject areas and are seldom used by general libraries. Some supply video, audio, and other materials as well as books or limit themselves to one or more of these special media. One may be best at supplying current bestsellers, while another focuses on finding out-of-the-way publications.

Vendors, whose business it is to supply books and other materials, can offer many benefits to libraries. By dealing in bulk, they can obtain discounts from publishers that can then be passed on to libraries even when only one copy of a title is being purchased. Those who have their own warehouses maintain a vast inventory from numerous publishers and can ship rapidly. Most are automated and can determine immediately the status of desired items. Most willingly tailor invoices to local needs, again assisted by automation. Most large vendors are tolerant of the vagaries of bureaucratic red tape and slow payment. Many offer an array of services that include regular reporting on outstanding orders, various forms of management reports, and quotes on request.

A good vendor will fight the library's battles for it, such as claiming and cajoling, proving previous payment, and other time-consuming tasks. In effect, the vendor's staff becomes an extension of the library's staff, making it doubly important to use stable, reliable vendors with competent employees.

Consolidation of orders for items from many publishers with one or several vendors saves the library time and money. Libraries mail orders in one envelope to one address; there is one place to deal with any problems; there is likely to be one service representative who knows the library's account well; and books arrive grouped in large boxes rather than packaged individually.

Most vendors employ sales representatives who make occasional visits to customer libraries, bringing news of recent developments, new services, special offers, and, often, statistics on the library's business with that vendor during the past year. These people are excellent sources of information; some of them are librarians, broadening their experience by working for a library supplier. In their use of librarians as staff members, their solicitation of and response to librarians' needs in the provision of information to the public, vendors are increasingly partners in the acquisitions process.

Some vendors supply only books, while others specialize in serials. Those who handle more than one type of material have separate departments, or even separate branches, for dealing with each type. Maintaining subscriptions is quite a different matter from obtaining a current monograph and requires specific expertise. Likewise, the out-of-print market is an entirely different game, best left to those who specialize in it.

Since warehousing is expensive, many vendors who deal in monographs do not maintain much inventory, limiting themselves to new books or to those that sell repeatedly. In most cases, the library places an order with the vendor, who must then place an order for the item with the publisher, thus increasing the time required to obtain a book. A vendor who accepts telephone or electronic orders and has a book in stock can often supply it in as little as two weeks. Nevertheless, even a vendor with a large inventory cannot stock at all times every book that might be wanted by any one of the libraries it deals with. The vendor is dependent on the publisher's ability to supply the books ordered. Books are often out of stock, and no one can obtain them until a sufficient supply has been printed and distributed. Such delays can vary from weeks to months. Other things can go wrong: books can be reported out of stock erroneously; publishers might ship the wrong book, the wrong edition, or the wrong format. An alert vendor will intercept such errors rather than pass them on to the library.

Most vendors in North America and Europe have automated databases that are available, in varying degrees, to the customers. At the very least, the vendor can be consulted by telephone and can check the database for the availability of given titles. Or the library may actually subscribe to the use of the database. Such services extend the library's access to information, contributing to the more rapid, accurate acquisition of materials.

A vendor will accept the library's order form and will ship quickly or report in a specified period of time and continue reporting at specified intervals until the order is filled or cancelled. Vendors commonly maintain a profile for each customer that specifies such preferences as invoice format, report interval, and length of time orders will remain open. Some book dealers also offer approval plans whereby they select and supply books based on library specifications regarding subject and publisher with various caveats on scope, format, etc. Such plans eliminate a great deal of detailed work that would be required to identify and prepare an order for each book. On the other hand, unless carefully monitored, these plans can result in unwanted material finding its way into the collection and desired material can be missed.

Serial vendors also maintain customer profiles, as well as recording information such as renewal schedules for periodicals. Some also supply subscriptions to CD-ROMs and other formats. Some will maintain standing orders on a customer-specified schedule such as every other year rather than every year. Management reports tailored to the library's needs, including fund accounting information, are often available as well. Periodicals are sold without discount, and a service charge is added. The amount of the service charge varies, as do the services provided. Again consolidation of orders is significant. One invoice from a vendor can renew hundreds or thousands of titles that would require separate invoices if each title were ordered directly from its publisher.

THE PARTNERSHIP

The relationship between librarians and vendors is a firm one. Librarians use vendors to obtain discounts, consolidate ordering, function as added staff, and provide a variety of services. Vendors form part of the increasingly complex and interconnected network that gets information to the library patron.

Vendors can supply libraries with useful data specific to a particular library's purchases, general data regarding actual and projected costs, and valuable data on the publishing industry. They can become partners in research projects and act as advocates in disputes. For instance, when high prices force librarians to cancel subscriptions, the vendor can so inform the publishers. Libraries should tell vendors what materials they need and how much they are willing to pay. Questionnaires from vendors should be answered carefully and promptly. Vendors use survey responses to gauge directions in which the library community is moving and to shape future research and development, products, seminar offerings, and the like. If libraries begin to change their approaches to collection development, vendors will have to adjust as well, adding new media and new services, preferably in anticipation of libraries' demands. My own experience indicates that questionnaires sent to vendors are given much greater attention than those sent to librarians. This is unfortunate because information exchange is crucial to developing and maintaining a viable partnership.

Vendors frequently make sudden reductions in approval plan coverage, continue to accept orders despite slow payment, and do other things that appear to be more in the interests of libraries than in their own interest. It is in their own interest, in the long run, to offer libraries the best prices and services possible, just as it is in libraries' interest to support good vendors by communicating with them, doing business with them, evaluating them, and refraining from making unreasonable requests, such as requests for the provision of numerous "free" services or excessive discounts. Few libraries can do without vendors, nor would libraries as a whole be served well by only one vendor. Variety is not only the spice of life, but also the sign of a healthy marketplace.

Partners though they may be, each has its own interests to protect. It is not a relationship without constraints, problems, and misunderstandings. The halcyon days of the 1960s and early 1970s when library markets were expanding, funding was plentiful for both books and staff, and currencies were relatively stable seem now but a distant, folkloric time. The difficulties of recent years—escalating prices, proliferating titles and formats, technological changes, and inadequate funding—have produced angry and demanding librarians, as well as vendors who feel caught in the middle between publisher and librarian.

Limited budgets, institutional regulations, and lack of knowledge about publishing and bookselling make the librarian a potentially difficult partner. Because of the large amount of esoteric material they purchase, research libraries are especially challenging partners. While librarians may demand higher discounts and more value-added services, publishers reduce their discounts to vendors. At the same time, librarians increasingly expect vendors to participate in forums, American Library Association (ALA) committees and discussion groups, speak at professional conferences, and generally carry on dialogues with the library community.

Vendors, however, are always aware that they are not library service organizations, but businesses whose success depends on making a profit. The company may be run by people who love books and are committed to access to information, but they must make money in order to survive.

For their part, librarians have not always been knowledgeable, evaluative, or sufficiently businesslike. It is important for librarians to be informed about publishing, know the policies, capabilities, and needs of their libraries, and recognize the vendors' abilities and how best to make use of them. We must know the impact of our demands on vendors and where our responsibility toward them lies. We must also understand the nature of the partnership that has developed largely as a result of our own demands. We must understand where partnership ends and abdication begins. If we set up an approval plan and simply let the books flow into the collection, never reviewing the profile or examining the books, we have abdicated our responsibility. Likewise, if a tape-loaded invoice is balanced and totalled by the library's automated system without examination of its line-by-line charges, we have something other than a partnership.

Joe Hewitt's recent article, "On the Nature of Acquisitions," is well worth careful study by all acquisitions librarians. He points out that "acquisitions work . . . tends to be undervalued and misunderstood," suffering from "a reputation for being predominantly routine, process-oriented, and relatively simple." In order to overcome this false image, the acquisitions librarian must become "an expert, [an] interpreter, and [a] counter-strategist in [the] complex relationship" between publishing and book distribution systems and libraries. This relationship between vendor and librarian is the focus of this book.

2 WHAT LIES AHEAD?

In the rapidly changing field of acquisitions librarianship, we have had to implement online systems, try to control spiralling costs and proliferating information, balance the acquisition and usage of new formats with old, and realize that our goal of building the ideal library collection is being transformed into one of providing access to information.

We can, to some extent, shape our technological and informational future. We have great power to shape the future relationship that will exist between acquisitions librarians and vendors. Librarians have too often been seen as reactive and lacking in vision. Impending changes in information acquisition and delivery could free librarians to become proactive participants in the information community. By forging new partnerships with suppliers, librarians will be able to spend less time on mundane activities—and will gain credibility and impact.

Is there a library in the developed world that has not seen the impact of technology? Remote research stations have had electronic access to the Agriculture Canada Library for years; small school libraries are replete with personal computers and CD-ROMs; OCLC has invaded special libraries. The future, however, may well rest on concepts that extend the uses of technology far beyond the reproduction of the catalog card in electronic format. This electronic future will radically alter the way information is disseminated—both the information that libraries obtain for patron use, and the information that libraries use internally to transact business. This future will change the very nature of what librarians do and, in particular, will change the relationship between acquisitions librarian and vendor.

TECHNICAL STANDARDS

Without standards of some sort, chaos reigns. In the field of electronic communication, lack of standards raises barriers and impedes the efficient flow of information. Standardization, on the other hand, enhances that flow.

In 1979, the International Standards Organization developed a model for ease of communication between systems of different manufacture called Open Systems Interchange (OSI). Numerous standards work together to permit information exchange between unlike systems. Otherwise incompatible systems are "open" to each other because they use the same technical standards for data transmission.

In the United States, the National Information Standards Organization (NISO) is the group responsible for approving technical standards relating to the information industry, including libraries, publishing, and bookselling. Under its aegis, the Book Industry Systems Advisory Committee (BISAC), the Serials Industry Systems Advisory Committee (SISAC), and other groups develop draft standards that eventually become official through NISO. Many standards are already in place, among them ISBN and ISSN, the Bookland EAN, which encodes the ISBN as a scannable bar code, and standards that make CD-ROMs usable on a variety of machines. One of SISAC's most notable recent achievements is the completion of a standard for the machine-readable issue and article level identifier for serials. This will permit scanning check-in as well as electronic article identification. Numerous standards exist, and more are constantly in development, dealing with everything from trade catalogs, indexes, order forms, serial title abbreviations, statistics, and serial holdings statements to common command language for online interactive systems. These standards affect libraries profoundly. Scannable issue identifiers in bar code form will not only enhance serial check-in, but also change the way it is done. Publishers, serials vendors, library systems vendors, and library personnel will all have to adapt.

ELECTRONIC DATA INTERCHANGE

One aspect of this trend toward standardization will have particular impact on acquisitions: electronic data interchange (EDI). The library community suffers from various incompatibilities. In acquisitions, one vendor's electronic ordering system will not order books from another vendor; status reports produced by a vendor's computer must be rekeyed into the library's acquisitions record; loading invoice or bibliographic tapes into a library system requires specific programming to link each system, vendor, and library; when migrating to a new online system, libraries face complex conversion of old data into the new environment, particularly for acquisitions and serials check-in files. The use of a uniform format for data will ease and speed the transaction of business, opening new avenues for service between vendor and library.

Electronic data interchange is the computer-to-computer communication of business data. Although the ideal would be one worldwide standard adhered to by all nations and industries, this is not currently the case. In the United States, the American National

Standards Institute Accredited Standards Committee, called X-12, has developed numerous standards that are used in a wide range of industries wherever American business interests predominate. The United Nations has begun to develop standards, and another set of standards was developed in the United Kingdom. Neither is compatible with X-12 standards, which are the most fully developed and widespread of the three.

X-12 is in wide use because it is flexible, fast, cost-effective, and applicable to any industry. Discount department stores, toy stores, supermarkets, and hardware stores use EDI. It is moving into the retail bookstore, and libraries cannot and should not be far behind. If libraries and their suppliers are to benefit from EDI, both must learn about it and become players in the field. Vendors and librarians can work together to shape their mutual future.

The same computer and the same format will link retail bookstores with publishers, wholesalers, and sidelines distributors. Once input, the original data will travel from computer to computer without further keying. Receipt of a shipment is as simple as scanning bar codes into the computer. This kind of uniform electronic ordering format should result in faster and more accurate delivery and increased profits. Waldenbooks, B. Dalton, Ingram, and Baker & Taylor are in the process of implementing X-12. The size and influence of these four mean that "the adoption of X-12 is inevitable for the book industry" (Mutter 1990).

Pubnet, an online ordering system used in bookstores, is committed to X-12. Technically, there is no reason why libraries could not also use this system, placing their own orders with publishers via computer. Whether either libraries or publishers would welcome such a development remains to be seen.

For libraries, the promise of X-12 is speed and ease of communication, computer to computer, freeing library staff and enhancing service. X-12 would permit library transactions of all kinds—including orders, claims, invoices, binding information, bibliographic information, etc.—to be exchanged rapidly and accurately between systems without rekeying or loading of magnetic tapes. Sources such as *Ulrich's* and *Books In Print* and vendor inventory files will be linked to library systems, allowing rapid location of information and creation and transmission of orders. By facilitating connections among libraries, vendors, and publishers, it will also give publishers accurate sales information more quickly, taking some of the guess work out of reprinting. Of course, some such communication takes place now, but EDI will permit that to happen much more easily and inexpensively, probably also increasing the level of detail provided.

EDI will also link libraries with the bureaucracies of which they are a part, other libraries, and other entities they do business with. It could mean the end of the paper order, the paper claim, the paper report, and the paper invoice.

It will mean enhanced data collection for statistical and analytical purposes. Instead of juggling management reports from various vendors and attempting to mesh them with the library's own data, all such information will pass through the library's online system. The result will be one amalgamated document. This will put at the library's disposal much data that is now either unavailable or so diverse that it is difficult to meld it into coherent and meaningful reports. EDI, combined with flexible online acquisitions systems and the capability for user designed reporting that exist now, should result in much finer analysis and understanding of expenditures, purchasing patterns, usage patterns, materials costs, and vendor performance, as well as sophisticated projections of expenditure and usage.

Given this potential, the question arises: What kind of information should be exchanged between library and vendor? And what might be done to provide types of service that do not now exist? Many of the services that vendors now provide for libraries concerning serials management and collection development will be enhanced. Of the questions asked of acquisitions personnel, one of the most difficult to answer is when a particular book is likely to arrive. However, retailers are looking forward to receiving online packing lists showing the shipping date and specific contents of cartons about to be shipped. With such lists, libraries, too, could then predict with some precision when a book might arrive. Add to this computer-to-computer transfer of status reports, and the future seems bright indeed to overworked staffs attempting to key in myriad reports in different formats or to transfer them to a paper order file.

Could not EDI expand the potential of approval plans? Electronic transfer of bibliographic records, including local fund codes, will become possible. Electronic informational transfer will also enhance profiles of collections, funds, and priorities, permitting changes to be swiftly incorporated. Similarly, information on books to be returned could be sent back to the vendor with the input of a simple code into the original bibliographic record.

Accounting results in tremendous duplication of effort. With electronic links to both publisher and library, the vendor could simplify accounting. One record would travel not only from vendor to library but also from library to local accounting office. Currently, bibliographic and billing data are very likely input by the publisher, again by the vendor, again by the library, and yet again by the agency that actually pays the library's bills.

All of this is ultimately based on the question: What do libraries want vendors to do for them? Vendors will be capable of doing much, much more for libraries than they do now. If developed carefully, new services can be the means to free librarians to participate more directly in the community they serve.

Libraries will demand services from vendors based on machine-to-machine communication. These and technological developments not yet on the horizon will unquestionably alter the relationship between libraries and vendors and will give them new venues for interaction. In the fast moving world of library automation, stages are passed quickly and new developments constantly make systems outmoded.

FULL TEXTS ONLINE

The computer undeniably provides rapid access to information by permitting users to search databases rapidly and to input requests from remote locations. In the end, though, what most users want is the information itself, often on a piece of paper. Libraries now give patrons a tantalizing and frustrating glimpse of what electronic access to information might mean. Online catalogs and CD-ROM indexes put citations in users' hands in a fraction of the time otherwise required. But the final step, obtaining the text itself, all too often becomes a saga of trips around library stacks; of material not on the shelf; of delays caused by waiting for access to materials caught in the compact shelving game, waiting to use photocopiers, or waiting while material is obtained through interlibrary loan.

Full-text document delivery and electronic publishing of various sorts promise the best of both worlds—and the bonus of permitting rapid access to the text desired. Only those materials needed will be provided in hard copy, and they will go directly to the user. The user will be freed from the chore of trying to find journals on the library shelf and then photocopying them. And the library will be freed from the purchase and maintenance of the same journals.

The above scenario is based on the concept of online access to the contents of printed journals, with the articles available in printed form for a fee. Other journals will not exist in printed form at all. In fact, today some 60 publishers in the United States alone produce journals in electronic form only—although such journals may still be available on paper on request. How a library subscribes to these journals, handles copyright and licensing issues, and whether it chooses to archive journals are major issues to be resolved.

An early experiment in full-text delivery is the ADONIS Project, on which there is a fairly lengthy bibliography. In this instance the full texts of all articles from 224 biomedical journals from 1987 and 1988 were made available on CD-ROM. Despite problems and limitations during the early stages of this project, it continues to be developed by Blackwell, Pergamon, Springer Verlag, and Elsevier and now includes over 300 journals.

Also on the frontier of information delivery is the CARL System, which provides online indexing of the contents of over 2,000 periodicals within hours of their receipt and equally rapid supply of texts. The goal of CARL is resource sharing through connecting sites and document supply. Many other full-text projects are being developed. Once exposed to such services, patrons may never again be satisfied with less.

Translating such promise into practice may not be easy. Which journals are most needed in this mode? The most heavily used or the least? Perhaps those containing critical, time-sensitive information such as medical publications will be provided online while less critical material may continue to be published in printed form. On the other hand, perhaps everyone's expectations will be raised so that, time sensitive or not, all kinds of information will be demanded online. Who will pay for the delivered document? How will all of this impinge on the materials budget and how will it affect suppliers of traditional materials? Will librarians influence the direction taken by electronic publishing?

Despite the potential of these technological developments for eliminating the printed word, there does not seem to be any expectation among librarians, publishers, or book distributors that printed materials will cease to exist any time soon. People like books and magazines. They like something printed to hold onto. Despite the growing popularity of electronic mail and electronic publishing, hard copy will still remain. The electronic future will be an add-on, not a replacement for the printed word. Nonetheless, that electronic future will challenge both librarians and vendors. In that future, the library patron may not even enter the library but may interact from home or office via computer with a variety of local and remote databases, will download and manipulate information, and will communicate with library staff members from the same computer. This, and even more, is the promise of the National Research and Education Network (NREN). Although its final form and funding remain unclear, should NREN become a reality, the futuristic scenario of total computer linkage for everyone with all information could become reality. Taken to its logical extreme, it means total connectivity (to the next desk, the library in the next town, the other side of the world) and completely seamless (i.e., invisible) connections locally and worldwide.

The foundation on which such connectivity will be built is a variety of technical standards. Ignorance of new developments and failure to deal with the difficult questions they pose may leave libraries out of the future, with all its promise. While keeping this promising, if demanding, future in mind, it may be useful to take a look, in the chapters ahead, at the vendor/librarian relationship today.

3 CHOOSING BOOK VENDORS

A truly equitable partnership depends on knowledge. In recent years, vendors have become increasingly knowledgeable about libraries. Librarians, however, have not become similarly informed about publishing and the role of vendors, nor do they normally base vendor selection decisions on hard data. Nevertheless, if one accepts the concept of a partnership between vendors and librarians, it seems obvious that librarians, as well as vendors, should carefully choose their partners.

VENDOR OR PUBLISHER?

The first questions to be asked are: What do vendors do for the library? What does a particular vendor do that makes it a justifiable choice? Is the vendor's service worth what it costs? There are really only two sources for library materials: the publisher or a vendor. Occasionally, a book store may be used if speed is essential. Although in most cases it is possible to buy materials directly from the publisher, most libraries choose to use vendors. The reasons for this are: 1. It is simpler and more efficient for the library to batch orders rather than to treat each one individually; and 2. Vendors provide services unavailable, or available to a lesser extent, from publishers.

Particularly in times of staff shortages, it is much more efficient to mail a group of 50 orders to one vendor, to deal with one vendor report, to open a few rather than 50 boxes, and to process a consolidated invoice, than to prepare and mail 50 envelopes, assimilate 50 reports, and process 50 invoices, resulting in the writing of 50 checks. This is not to say that a library must use only one vendor for all orders, but that batching of orders for selected, proven vendors is considerably more efficient than individual processing of one order for each item wanted.

Although few publishers target the library market, many vendors do. Since publishers seldom offer discounts on single-item orders, the vendor may be able to offer a better price than the publisher. However, libraries or library systems that order large quantities of popular titles well in advance of publication can save time and receive discounts from the publishers. Vendors offer a range of services and a consolidated source of information no publisher can match. Vendors maintain extensive files on publishers, including policies, addresses, distributors, etc. These files are constantly updated. A vendor will advise a customer of such things as price increases, non-returnable situations, and different formats. Vendors supply regular reports on open orders, sometimes tailoring the format of the report to the library's specifications. Publishers are usually less accommodating.

In some cases, the choice is made by publishers who decree that their materials are obtainable only directly from them. Like it or not, librarians must deal with these publishers. In these cases, it is prudent to become familiar with the publishers' policies and quirks, since only a few will accommodate themselves to the library. Imagine what would happen if one of the largest scholarly publishers, most of whose books are purchased by all academic libraries and whose books are found in virtually every library in North America, decided to do only direct sales. Academic libraries, most of which obtain these materials on approval plans, would find those plans suddenly disrupted. They would face an overwhelming addition to and disruption of daily work flow if these books had to be selected and ordered direct from the publisher. Meanwhile, the publisher after first being bombarded with library complaints would be inundated with thousands of orders, if libraries could handle the increased work load.

Could publishers handle the distribution? Could they provide tape-loaded records comparable to those provided by the approval vendor? Would they tolerate the idiosyncrasies of libraries and their bureaucracies such as slow payment and special invoicing requirements? The prospect is nightmarish. On the other hand, some publishers, while not *requiring* direct orders, offer incentives to encourage customers to place orders directly, resulting in prices that are lower than can be obtained through vendors. Some are sufficiently aware of the library market, providing capable customer service representatives and truly useful incentives, so that dealing with them is a positive experience. If this is the case, and incentives will not be obviated by increased staff time spent in dealing with problems, it may be in the library's interest to order direct.

Buying direct must have limits. If every publisher offered an incentive plan for libraries to buy direct, the increased workload for libraries would be incalculable. Moreover, publishers incur costs related to direct distribution programs, which are likely to result in higher prices for books.

In addition, they are taking business away from their distributors, not a common occurrence in other industries. Certain exceptions to the use of vendors offer some advantages to libraries, but in general using them makes sense.

It is important to note that specialty vendors, rather than general ones, may best serve certain special libraries such as medical or law libraries. Specialized vendors who target the library market and truly understand it are often the best sources of subject-specific materials, special formats such as microfilm or government documents. Such vendors are well known to art, music, medical, law, documents and other librarians who purchase highly specialized material.

DISCOUNTS AND COST-PLUS PRICING

The more welcome side of vendors' fees is the discount. Although discounts have become embedded in the process of providing books to libraries, there is no logical reason why this should be so. Libraries are retail buyers, and as such might be expected to pay full list price. They should realize that and accept the discounts they get with grace rather than demanding more.

The library must understand the discount schedule of its vendors. A discount may be contractual or may be less formal. Even under a statewide contract, some libraries negotiate a better rate for themselves. Since a vendor can only put into a statewide contract an average discount, the smaller accounts will benefit the most. The larger customers will find themselves on the short end of the discount scale and may do better negotiating on their own.

Libraries that distribute their orders among several vendors, giving a similar mix to all, may prefer a fixed discount rate rather than a book-by-book discount. This is a somewhat controversial approach, since, in one view, it is offered only because it benefits the vendor through a guaranteed volume of orders. The fixed discount can certainly be risky if not approached in a knowledgeable manner. It is essential to know present discounts, as well as present and likely future ordering patterns. It may be possible to negotiate separate flat rates for specific types of material with different vendors. Some libraries target their orders to specific vendors based on expected discount and/or service, but do not enter into any fixed agreement.

Librarians sometimes seem to suffer from "discount greed," demanding discounts beyond what is reasonable while at the same time demanding ever more free services. In many cases, the stringent financial policies of the library's institution forces such an attitude. Nevertheless, unless it makes a reasonable profit, a vendor will not last long. There is a limit to how much discount each vendor can allow and still make money. While librarians must carefully balance the relative importance of discount and service, it behooves vendors to run as tight a ship as possible, to be honest about their costs, and to offer the best discounts they can afford. Even a vendor whose service is excellent will fall from grace if a librarian begins to suspect excessive prices.

The discount a vendor provides on any given book depends on the discount it receives from the publisher. Certain publishers normally give significant discounts on large orders, which vendors, supplying numerous customers, are able to take advantage of. The largest discounts are on trade titles, where vendors may receive 40 percent to 50 percent off the list price. However, much of what vendors sell carries a far lower discount, and sometimes none. Many titles are sold to vendors at a 30 percent to 33 percent discount. Scholarly books may carry a 20 percent discount, while many books aimed at the library market are discounted only 5 percent to 15 percent, and most association publications are not discounted at all. If a vendor needs to make 22 percent in order to survive, it is obvious that it cannot offer any discount on a book for which it receives 20 percent or less and, in fact, will have to add a service charge in order to bring the price into an acceptable range.

To some extent, the trade titles can "carry" the others, with their larger profit margin offsetting losses on other types of books. However, vendors often prefer each title to pay for itself rather than gamble on a high volume of trade titles. They want a good mix of titles between the profitable and the less so. This enhances their chances of making a profit while still allowing the customer to receive some discounts.

Every vendor has an established procedure for pricing each book, based on the price it must pay the publisher and including other factors, such as contract requirements of the customer. Different customers may pay different prices for the same title.

The ultimate price a vendor charges a library for a book need not be based on discount—that is, working down from the discount provided to the vendor by the publisher. An alternate method, cost-plus pricing, works up from the actual price paid by vendor to publisher. In this method, amounts are added to the price paid to cover the vendor's expenses and to provide a profit margin. However logical this may seem, it does not appear to be as common as discount pricing. Libraries like discounts and most vendors' procedures have been developed on this basis. Either method should yield comparable prices if the vendors correctly calculated margins and are not overcharging libraries.

Librarians and vendors need each other and should put every effort into facilitating the flow of information from publisher to user. Vendors play a significant role in this flow because they are the distributors for the publishers. Without an efficient means of distribution, publishers would sell few books and libraries would be hard-pressed to provide patrons with needed information. One significant way in which vendors aid the flow of books from publisher to reader is through approval plans, which guarantee a certain level of sales. The books go ultimately to numerous customers, although the publisher ships one large quantity to the vendor.

VALUE-ADDED SERVICES

Beyond the basics, vendors have devised numerous services intended to assist not only the acquisitions librarian but the selector as well. Certain vendors have long offered prebound, fully cataloged and processed books; catalog cards; and leasing arrangements. As librarians' professional responsibilities became more demanding, they looked to vendors for help; at about the same time, library automation burgeoned. Vendors with automated databases could do wonders for a library. They supply bibliographic information in various formats, including bibliographies of new books, approval slips, and notices of "specials," in the form of lists, on forms, and on magnetic tape. Such notifications can often be limited to specified subjects and formats. Vendors can be asked not to duplicate a title on approval or standing order, and most will tailor invoices to the library's needs. They can produce open order reports on automated systems and provide them as the library specifies. They will often schedule shipments to mesh with the library's work flow.

As vendors developed technologically advanced products, demand increased. Libraries demanded standards, tape loads into diverse systems, and interfaces—all free. These value-added services, however, are costly to provide. Unless the costs are recovered directly, they reduce profit. There is a limit to how much a company can absorb and remain viable.

Vendors also provide many other services—toll-free telephone numbers, visits by sales representatives, booths at ALA, hospitality suites, and monetary support for a local conference. The list is long. These services represent costs, and they must be paid for.

Vendors will often bend over backward to keep a good customer happy, accepting returns that were the result of library error and waiting patiently for payment that must make its way through a bureaucracy over which the library has no control. Vendors have even agreed to continue supplying books to libraries whose funding has been cut off, amounting to thousands of dollars they know will not be paid anytime soon. Such policies must have their limits, though, if the vendor is to survive.

In summary, some publishers adopt a "take or leave it" attitude toward library customers, whereas those vendors who serve the library market go to great lengths to give libraries the pricing and services they want.

PRICE VS. SERVICE

How can a librarian obtain the best price and best service? The acquisitions librarian controls what goes into the collection by choice of vendor. If a group of books can be obtained at a discount of 37 percent, the savings can be used to purchase additional items for the collection. On the other hand, if a vendor offering a discount fails to supply the materials, the library may never acquire them, and may even incur considerable expense in the attempt.

"No frills" booksellers may be able to offer higher discounts because they do not have the expenses of providing a variety of services such as notification slips and information on magnetic tape. If accurate supply of books is the primary need of the library—and service features are secondary—"no frills" vendors may be the best choice.

Best price and best service do not always go hand in hand. Choices must be made on individual orders or groups of orders. Sometimes speed will outweigh all other factors, making the local full-price bookstore the preferred source.

MAKING THE CHOICE

The question then becomes: Which vendors and why? This is where few libraries can produce hard data to justify their choices.

Given the pressures of each work day, systematic, in-depth vendor evaluation falls by the wayside. Vendor evaluation will be discussed more fully later, but when auditors or irate patrons or other vendors raise the issue, the acquisitions librarian should have some idea of why particular vendors are used. Are books supplied promptly, in good condition, at an acceptable price? Are reports regular, clear, and accurate? Are invoices accurate, legible, and presented in the desired format and desired number of copies? Has another vendor demonstrated failure in any of these areas? Are other desired services provided? Are vendors given a chance to be heard, or is the acquisitions librarian's mind closed to all but a select few favorites? Is habit the primary selection criterion?

IDENTIFYING VENDORS

It is worthwhile to consider how one learns about potential vendors. Although it often seems that every vendor on earth wants to "come by for a little chat," especially where a sizeable budget is concerned, occasionally the time is well spent. Some publications are useful. *Literary Market Place*, for example, lists book wholesalers along with a wealth of other information relevant to the publishing industry. An alphabetical list of vendors includes full names and addresses. Vendors are also grouped by type of activity, "approval plans," "accounts, libraries," "government publications," etc. Another way to locate appropriate vendors is to query other libraries in depth about their needs and how well particular vendors meet them. Libraries with automated systems may have printouts of vendors' names and addresses that they will be willing to share. Libraries that are agencies of states with multiple vendor book contracts may be willing to share the part of the contract listing vendor names and addresses. Attendance at the American Library Association annual meeting, and meetings of other groups such as the Special Libraries Association, will expose one to a wide range of vendor exhibits.

Identifying foreign vendors can be more challenging, although major foreign vendors who court the North American market make their presence known. Latin America, Asia, Africa, the Caribbean, and some areas of Europe, present perennial problems for acquisitions departments. Even if little is purchased from these areas, it is best to be prepared. A reference shelf of photocopied articles, comments by other librarians, publications of the Seminar on the Acquisition of Latin American Library Materials (SALALM), and records of one's own dealings with foreign vendors can prove invaluable when ordering from abroad. A particularly useful reference is the *Directory of Vendors of Latin American Library*

Materials. Another is the *Directory of Foreign Monograph Vendors Serving Libraries in North Carolina*, which lists 147 North American and foreign vendors, with indexes by country and language of publication.

Foreign vendors exhibit at the American Library Association annual meeting, as well as the American Booksellers Association annual meeting. Attendance at the Frankfurt Book Fair (and other fairs outside North America) are not only a source of information on vendors, but offer insights into publishing and book distribution. Latin American vendors attend SALALM annual meetings. Personal contact is important in building partnerships with these suppliers.

NARROWING THE FIELD

If an untried vendor is under consideration, the vendor should be queried in detail. All vendors will provide names of other customers. Calls to libraries with budgets and purchasing patterns similar to one's own can elicit useful information regarding the vendor's service.

If a library collects heavily in specific areas, it is wise to explore in depth exactly what vendors can do in supplying that material. Librarians should ask whether that material is warehoused and how extensively, whether there are problems with certain publishers, and whether the vendor specializes in desired subject areas. Probing, specific questions are the key to obtaining information on which to choose a vendor.

Following is a list of suggested questions adapted from one provided by a North American vendor:

- Where is the company located?
- How old is it?
- What is its financial condition?
- How many employees are there?
- What is their training and experience?
- What are the names, addresses, and phone numbers of other customers?
- Who will provide references?
- Is there a specific person within the company to handle your account?
- Do you have documentation of your services?
- Are there company representatives who visit the library at regular intervals?
- What are your policies (i.e., pricing, reporting, returns, invoicing, cancellations)?

- What is the cost of the services provided?
- How is vendor/librarian communication handled?
- How much stock, if any, is warehoused? What types of books are kept in inventory?
- Is the company a full-service or specialized vendor?
- Will you discuss issues of concern to the library community?
- Do you participate in forums for the discussion of such issues (e.g., conferences, standards committees)?
- Do you participate in the development of standards, coordination with library system vendors, and joint projects with libraries?

A similar list should be developed by every library whenever it is selecting vendors. Each library should develop a policy concerning vendor versus direct ordering, so that each order passes through a process of filtration that directs it to the expected best source of supply.

FOREIGN VS. NORTH AMERICAN

There are few differences among the major foreign and North American vendors of library books. All are players in the same game and know the value of automation, the universality of the MARC format, the necessity for standards, the need to keep customers happy in a constantly changing market. All maintain representatives in North America, visit their North American customers, and/or exhibit at ALA. Generally, a vendor situated in its own country will best understand the publishing scene and means of doing business there and will often obtain the best price for an item. Although many British publications are readily available in North America, this is not true of other foreign books. This is why many libraries have long subscribed to the idea of purchasing in country of origin.

One must consider also the currency in which the vendor must be paid. Vendors accustomed to serving the North American library market will accept payment in dollars, but small publishers may not. When faced with a supplier who demands payment in local currency, libraries can waste staff time and incur added expense trying to convince the supplier to accept dollars or having the library's check converted at a local bank. Or the library may have to ask a vendor to pay on its behalf and bill it for the service. If direct orders are necessary to third world countries, a letter is likely to be more effective than a computer-produced form, especially if one writes in the native language. Understanding how business is conducted in a given country is invaluable, as is the personal visit for those who collect seriously enough to justify it. Extra effort must go into understanding, accommodating, and developing relationships with third world suppliers, but it will be well worth the effort if your goal is to build a useful collection.

The price advantage of buying in country of origin may be lost in the move to a world economy as evidenced by the development of the European Community and the creation of global publishing houses. European currencies will tend to move as a block once the European Community becomes a reality. In such a market, will localized vendors disappear and the major ones assume a wider role? There may be European vendors rather than French vendors or Italian ones. However, it will ultimately be the libraries who decide, by where they place their orders, which vendors survive. And, indeed, service may well remain superior in country (or perhaps continent) of origin. If librarians value and reward service and foster close working relationships with superior vendors, these vendors should endure, no matter what changes occur in publishing or in national economies.

Just deciding what is a foreign title is not always easy these days. Is any title distributed in North America defined as North American, even though some have been published abroad and may be cheaper if purchased abroad? Most British books of interest to North American readers are also published on this side of the Atlantic, generally within several months of their publication in Britain, and may be cheaper than their British counterparts. Moreover, North American books will probably be supplied at a discount, whereas British books are not. If money were the sole concern, libraries might stop buying British books. But how does one identify and track the British books needed in North American editions? Are libraries willing to wait for the North American edition? How does one deal with the possibility that the North American edition may differ from the British? How does one pick up those that do not appear in North America? And if libraries all but sever relations with British vendors, will those vendors be there at some future date when situations change and North American libraries really need them? Is speed of delivery or a lower price preferable? How much lower? While not all libraries may need to consider these questions in detail, they should be aware of them and of the impact of such choices on budgets and staff.

Selecting vendors from some areas such as Latin America, Asia, Africa, the Caribbean, and parts of Europe is always challenging and can be frustrating. Nevertheless, the same principles of vendor selection, evaluation, and treatment apply. Sometimes special requests may be made by vendors who are encountering difficulties

SUMMARY
Steps to a viable partnership:

1. Know institutional policies and objectives.
2. Vendor vs. publisher.
3. Consider discount, pricing policies, and service charges.
4. How many vendors?
5. Which vendors?
6. Communicate.
7. Evaluate.

in their own countries. They may want their checks made out in a certain way or sent to a different address. But if they can get the books and provide reasonable service they should be accommodated. Some major North American vendors have branches in other areas of the world and are worth using for any material they can provide.

One must maintain records of "problem" vendors so the same company will not be used again in the future. Librarians must also keep records on rarely used but acceptable vendors. If a library orders only two or three books year published in, say, Jerusalem, it is still necessary to know to whom to send orders and what has been done in the past. If two Israeli vendors have been used, their names, addresses, and a record of their performance on even a few orders must be accessible.

HOW MANY VENDORS?

Each library must decide how many vendors to use and for which materials and whether particular vendors are worth what they cost. Will a library select a number of good North American vendors, using past experience as a guide, or simply choose them at random as a test, sending this week's orders to the first on the list, next week's orders to the next? Or do they target each order to the vendor most likely to supply it quickly and at the best price? This is the approach used at the University at Albany Libraries with successful results. Does the library want to simplify ordering to the point of using only one vendor for all North American titles? Putting all orders in one vendor's computer carries with it the same potentials for disaster as putting all eggs in one basket, especially as the size of the budget increases.

THE CHOICE IS THE LIBRARY'S

The cost of a book vendor is the sum of many things—the amount of discount, the number of errors, service charges. Each library must make its own judgment about vendors. The process of choosing and using book vendors is complex: communication with vendors, awareness of markets and currency changes, use of automation, institutional mandates, and the like make assigning an order to a vendor anything but an automatic process.

4 CHOOSING SERIALS VENDORS

Suppliers of serials function quite differently from book vendors because they are essentially selling service rather than bibliographic items. They are partners with the library to an even greater extent than book jobbers, because of the ongoing nature of each order. This fact, plus the large sums of money involved, and the vagaries of serial publications themselves make the relationship between a serials vendor and the library much more complex than that between book jobber and library. It is therefore especially important to choose carefully in this area. While it is often difficult to obtain hard data on which to base a decision, it is not impossible to evaluate price and service when selecting a supplier, and it is somewhat easier to evaluate one currently in use.

PERIODICALS

VENDOR OR PUBLISHER?

As with books, one must decide whether to use a jobber or buy directly from the publisher. The same points in favor of consolidating monograph orders with a vendor apply in the case of serials: added efficiency and services. Three-quarters of the institutional subscriptions in this country, totalling well over a billion dollars annually, are handled by subscription agencies.

The role of the subscription agent has changed considerably over the years. There was a time when periodicals were sold to agents at a discount, just as books are. In turn, agents sold subscriptions to libraries, often at a discount, and made a profit without adding service charges, just as book jobbers often do today. Over the years, publishers reduced or eliminated discounts to subscription agents, and they continue to do so. Faced with disappearing discounts, subscription agents had to establish an acceptable profit margin for themselves in order to remain in business. The only way to do this was to add a service charge. Then some libraries moved subscriptions away from agents and ordered directly from the publishers, while other libraries began to ask for services, not just periodical issues. Thus, the modern subscription agent was born, caught with libraries in a net woven of services, fees, and ever-rising prices.

Before discussing in detail the services made available by subscription agents and how libraries pay for them, let us consider what a modern subscription agent does. To quote John Merriman, "The agent should be the expert who relieves the library of a large administrative load by providing a convenient and reliable method of procuring journals from all parts of the world." As Merriman also points out, this is based on "mutual trust between librarian, agent and publisher" and will fail without both trust and integrity. This is the ideal of the subscription agent who will act as go-between, relieving the librarian's burdens, and whose staff functions as an extension of the library's staff, saving time and money, always in short supply in libraries.

The large proportion of subscriptions handled by agents attests to the widespread belief in this ideal. Rare indeed is the serials department that places all subscriptions directly with publishers. Far too much staff time, it is believed, would go into the maintenance of so many individual orders. Generally, only small lists are handled in this way. While efficiency can be realized by batching orders and by processing few rather than many invoices and checks, there are other considerations.

Those subscription agencies that want a given library's business may make extravagant promises—low service charge, numerous services, conscientious customer service representatives, flawless start-up, changeover, and billing. Before responding to such promises, the library must decide what it wants the supplier to do, as opposed to what the library prefers to do for itself. Some librarians believe that a subscription agent is best used for ordering the most straightforward material that is obtainable with little difficulty. Others use suppliers for the "headache" titles that result in lengthy telephone bills and thick folders of correspondence. In fact, easy material is easy for anybody, librarian or agent, and problems are problems no matter who handles them. A library with a sufficiently knowledgeable staff might deal with problematic material itself. The library will spend considerable time and effort communicating with the vendor anyway. The vendor does not "do it all"; in fact, little or nothing is done without instructions from the customer. So, one must decide whether the letters, phone calls, fax messages, claims, and so on *that will be necessary no matter who supplies the order* are best sent to an agent or to a publisher. Sound decisions of this sort can only be based on experience and knowledge and will vary with the library.

Some librarians believe that attempting to find one's way through this maze is not cost-efficient in terms of staff time. However, where materials budgets are separate from salaries and materials budgets are inadequate, saving staff time at the expense of the materials budget is not likely to find institutional support. This is particularly true in these times of overwhelming price increases in serials.

Although some publishers do target the library market and offer programs and services that are worthwhile, they must be judged with care. Similarly, memberships in organizations that offer price breaks on publications are often best handled directly, although sometimes these price advantages are obtainable even when the membership is with an agent. There are indeed times when direct ordering is advantageous, and it is up to each library to determine this based on knowledge of local needs, publishers, and vendors.

It is not difficult to collect librarians' complaints about unacceptable behavior by publishers who take on the library market directly. Many of these complaints center around aggressive sales practices and inept account management. Sales people who are overly persistent, who make and retract verbal promises, who offer prices lower than the prices eventually billed, and who ship based on tenuous assumptions raise the ire of acquisitions librarians. Should the library return items shipped in such a scenario, the salesperson may cry that he or she will be fired—a desperate attempt indeed to finalize a sale.

Inability to understand and accommodate library needs is also common among such suppliers. When told that the library requires the supplier's Federal Employee Identification Number, a supplier may refuse to do business with the institution. Others may claim not to have such a number. If they do accept a library customer, the account may be poorly managed. Libraries have been talked into paying several years in advance at a reduced rate only to be dunned in subsequent years because the supplier could not keep track of the advance payment.

Like books, periodicals may be purchased from general or special-market subscription agents. Very often the specialized agent is the best choice for the special library since it can concentrate its efforts on providing in-depth coverage of the field.

When deciding where to place subscriptions, consider staffing levels and expertise as well as in-house automation capabilities. If staff is plentiful and capable, it makes less sense to use a vendor. Likewise, making extensive use of a vendor who produces myriad management reports is redundant if the same or even better ability exists in house.

Ideally, the actual source or sources of a library's periodicals represents the end product of a process of filtration and should be subject to periodic review.

VENDOR SELECTION AND USE

Once the library decides to use a subscription agent, it must find an agent that can best provide it with basic services: speedy start-up of new subscriptions; prompt, effective response to all communication; accurate billing in accord with the library's requirements; and renewal of subscriptions with publishers per the library's instructions. In addition, the vendor must supply special services required by the library. The specific titles desired will affect the choice of supplier; the best source for a medical list will likely not be the best choice for a law list.

Subscription agents can be identified in the same general ways as book vendors: collecting information from published sources, at meetings, and from other libraries. An indispensable resource is *International Subscription Agents* (American Library Association).

There are far fewer choices among subscription agents than among book jobbers. Even among librarians, serials have a reputation of being sources of endless trouble. Why should they be any easier for vendors to handle? A successful seller of serials needs special expertise, including knowledge of a vast array of serial publishers; ability to track suspensions, cessations, rebirths, and changes of titles and publisher. It must deal with the often changeable policies of both publishers and libraries. Today, this means a substantial investment in a sophisticated automated system and capable personnel. Moreover, the market is static at best, if not actually shrinking, and the profit margin is low. Thus, it is not surprising that there are few companies in the business.

Nevertheless, choosing among subscription agents is not made easier by the paucity of their numbers. Whereas book jobbers can set forth discount schedules, average delivery times, return policies, warehousing, postage and handling fees and the like in a fairly straightforward manner, similar discussions with serial vendors can do little to shed light where it is most needed. If a library wants only the essentials listed above—no frills—it must find an agent who supplies just that. Such a library, subscribing through a vendor who offers much more, will pay for those unwanted additional services.

A library with simple, clearly defined objectives and the will to ignore proffered frills is fortunate. It can, and should, query similar libraries with similar needs who are currently customers of vendors under consideration, question the vendor in some detail, and explore both price and service charge. Harry Kuntz provides an extensive list of items to be explored with a prospective subscription agent such as services, management, facilities, and fiscal condition, and suggests various sources from which data may be assembled. Indeed, this is what all libraries, no matter what they expect from a subscription agent, should do.

Each vendor will claim to have the lowest prices, the most favorable exchange rates, the best service, and the most knowledge of the markets. The only way for the librarian to make an intelligent decision is to become knowledgeable about vendors. It may be useful to consider three areas in which wild claims are made, often obscuring the real issues: prices, services, and service charges.

Prices

Although it is commonly assumed that the base price of periodicals does not vary among suppliers, this is not necessarily the case because publishers may set differential subscription rates; postage fees may or may not be included; and exchange rates will influence the price of foreign titles. Vendors can be queried as to how base price is determined, and comparative prices can be sought for a sample list for a given completed year. Be sure to ask what exactly is in the database from which the price is derived. Did it include supplementary charges, or was it the original price charged, with added charges not shown? Agents have been known to bid low prices by using such incomplete or outdated information.

If comparative price quotes are needed for a monograph, they can be obtained fairly quickly via telephone or telefacsimile. Trying to pin down the price of a one-year subscription to a periodical six months before that year begins, or even after it begins, is a virtual impossibility. Even trying to establish comparative actual costs for *completed* years is a daunting task. There are varying pricing, billing, and reporting practices among vendors, and publishers often raise prices at the start of the year, even after prices have been announced and vendors have paid them. Even in a bid situation, it is not possible to know firm prices, because allowances will be made for subsequent price increases by publishers. Only after a subscription year is over can one see in one's own records what a given title truly cost. In order to compare pricing among vendors, one would then need to query a library subscribing to the same title(s) from another vendor the total price paid, without service charge. In this way, admittedly time-consuming, some comparative data on *completed* years could be assembled. Relative pricing patterns might be assumed to hold true for current years as well, at least for North American titles.

As problematic as serials in general have been in recent years, foreign titles have presented even more difficulties. Merely deciding where to obtain foreign serials can be an exercise in frustration because of complexities of currency fluctuations and questions of service to distant markets. North American vendors dealing in foreign titles claim to offer the lowest prices and best service despite their distances from the sources. They point to their ability to play the currency markets and to their own European offices. Meanwhile, foreign vendors point out that they have had many years of personal contact with the publishers in their countries, and that they too buy currencies in order to secure favorable rates.

How, then, does one distribute subscriptions in a rational way? A library may choose to place all orders with one vendor, to place subscriptions with vendors in country of origin, or to systematically split the list. The library must weigh the relative importance of price and service. Country of origin purchasing has long been favored and has yet to be disproved, despite the movement of North American vendors into the European arena. All major vendors stockpile currencies other than their own in an attempt to hedge against inflation. How well any vendor foresees its customers' future needs and tailors its internal pricing policies to fit, will determine which vendor offers the lowest price. Since only hindsight and considerable research will reveal who this was, the librarian must focus instead on overall performance. Advantageous pricing combined with superior service *can* be found.

Services

The maze of services offered grows constantly. The library community has demanded many of these services—and continues to demand them "free." Librarians have been too little aware of the costs to the companies and to themselves of the products they have demanded, for nothing is truly free. In addition, these services frequently place additional burdens elsewhere—such as on the library's staff.

The proliferation of computer-based services began in the 1960s, when most subscription agents began to automate their records. Following is a composite list of services offered by several subscription agents:

- Ordering and renewal (automatic or otherwise, at the library's specification) of any serial, promptly and accurately;
- Quick and efficient claims handling;
- Regular response to claims;

- Batching subscriptions for common expiration date;
- Automatic merging of new orders with existing list;
- Prompt cancellations;
- Single annual renewal invoice;
- Maintenance of title file with bibliographic information on publications, data on publishers, payment data;
- Printed catalog;
- Catalog on microfiche;
- Ability to order titles not in the catalog or database;
- Price quotations;
- Sample copies;
- Back issues;
- Reprints;
- Out-of-print search service;
- Supply of formats other than print;
- Multiple-year subscriptions for reduced price;
- Trouble-free handling of subscriptions transferred from other vendors;
- Regular reporting on changes of title and frequency, delayed publications, etc.;
- Personal account service;
- Maintenance of and adherence to the library's special instructions;
- Maintenance of good working relationships with publishers;
- Prepayment to publishers in various currencies;
- Single annual renewal invoice;
- Convenient payment terms;
- Prepayment plans with resulting cost savings to the library;
- Customized invoicing;
- Separate invoicing by library-designated fund code;
- Invoices supplied on magnetic tape or diskette;
- Input of library-specific data such as fund codes and routing information into the database;
- Various customized management reports;
- Distribution of price increase projections and multiple year pricing surveys to customers;
- Publication of statistical data and analyses in professional journals.

The following additional services are available for a fee:

- Access to the vendor's online database;
- Online claiming;

- Serials management system, microcomputer or mainframe based, offering check-in, claiming, labelling, routing, binding, patron inquiry, holdings, and union lists;
- Conversion assistance;
- Electronic mail;
- Subscription and billing information on diskette for in-house manipulation with a spreadsheet program;
- Bibliographic interfaces with library systems;
- Index/abstract services;
- Access to various specialized online database files.

Many libraries use some of these services; few, if any use them all, but all share in paying for their existence. No doubt some who use them could survive without them and some who find them useful at some point will not need them at another time, such as when their own automation capabilities expand. One must carefully assess the cost and value to one's own library of each service. If use is to be made of a given service, time must be spent in doing so, staff must be trained, use of it integrated into work routines, and so on. If a report arrives only to be put on a shelf to collect dust, it is not worth having. Moreover, flaws may be found in a service: data may not correspond to the library's fiscal year. Or the vendor may report on bills issued or payment received during a given period of time, while the library needs data on money it actually spent during that period.

Examine these offerings carefully when choosing a vendor. Although each library will have its own needs, most would accept the first seven items as essential. The next, maintenance of a title file, would seem a prerequisite to performing any of the essentials. The next thirteen items would certainly be of use to some libraries, at some times. A printed catalog is a convenience that is often taken for granted. The annual catalogs produced by most serials suppliers are useful resources. They set forth the company's policies and services as well as providing a list of available titles and information about them such as ISSN, country of origin, current volume number, frequency, existence of title page and index, price, reduced rates for multiple year subscriptions, where indexed, etc.

The list of titles may be consulted when an order is contemplated, but the preceding text in these catalogs is often ignored. Nevertheless, here one will find much essential information. The catalog will explain how to order, transfer, and cancel titles, and list options for renewing and billing. If a stated policy is not to a library's liking, discussion of it should precede order placement. When establishing an account, options should be understood and choices clearly stated in writing. Changes should also be written, both for the vendor's and the library's benefit. However, as with all catalogs, title and pricing information is out of date the day it is printed. When a catalog is used, one must not forget that more current information may be available elsewhere, such as in *Ulrich's Plus* (Bowker) or through a telephone call to the vendor.

Price quotations and sample copies can be useful in making decisions. It is also helpful when an agent supplies back issues or reprint editions of titles currently received on subscription, or searches for out-of-print volumes. But these are not the only ways to complete runs of periodical titles. In these days of proliferating formats, it is almost necessary for a subscription agent to supply serials in various formats, as well as to supply available titles not included in the catalog.

Offering multiple-year subscriptions in order to take advantage of lower yearly rates has been popular for some time and is more easily managed in an automated environment than in a manual one. However, in recent years the savings realized from multiple-year subscriptions have diminished. Moreover, as serial prices have escalated, libraries with multiple-year subscriptions have been unable to effect cancellations to cut costs. Since few publishers accept mid-subscription cancellations, libraries undergoing large-scale examination of their lists—and equally large-scale cancellation projects—will benefit from single year subscriptions.

Most vendors have difficulty handling lists of transferred titles. Individual transfers often go smoothly enough. To some extent, the success of transfers depends on the library: the accuracy of the data it supplies to the new vendor and the lead time provided. To some extent, it depends on the expertise of the vendor. And to some extent, it depends on the publisher. Horror stories about the transfer of entire lists abound and are filled with lost subscriptions, missing issues, duplication, and billing nightmares.

The next three items on the list—regular reporting on changes, personal account service, and use of the library's special instructions—have come to be expected by almost every customer of every subscription agent. Nevertheless, the vendor can only report what it knows—and sometimes the customer knows it first—and personal account service is only as good as the person providing it. In short, such services will not solve all problems, or eliminate the need for alert, competent staff, nor should they be expected to. Input of the special needs of customers into an existing database is commonly taken for granted, but this is an expense for the vendor and should be used only if necessity dictates. If a library needs only three copies of each invoice, why go on accepting four?

The vendor's relationship to publishers is crucial to the success of the partnership. In fact, vendors form part of a tripartite partnership, which includes both libraries and publishers. They expend considerable time, effort, and money to maintain smooth relations with publishers. Part of this is a willingness to pay them in their own currencies.

Invoicing and payment often cause great consternation to both vendor and library. The vendor and librarian may see themselves as allied against the library bureaucracy in an effort to get an invoice paid. Subscription agents have been remarkably tolerant of situations in which they are unable to get consistent answers; fly personnel long distances for meetings that do not take place; wait months for payment, not knowing whether to pay publishers; and borrow money while awaiting promised payment. Despite this—and perhaps because the majority of their clients are not of such ilk—they continue to offer numerous invoicing services designed not only to help libraries but also to facilitate payment.

When vendors are willing and able to provide invoices in formats and numbers that one's institution requires and that make the staff's work easier, libraries are quick to make use of them. But there are pitfalls here too. In order for a vendor to input fund codes, the library must supply them accurately for each title, and someone on the vendor's staff must then input them accurately. If they are changed, the library must notify the vendor to make the change. This is the only way reports based on them can approach accuracy.

The single annual renewal invoice is a myth, given the necessity for supplementary billings to cover price increases. Of course, any new subscriptions established during a given year will be invoiced separately until they can be rolled into the annual renewal. With large lists, the sheer size of the annual billing detracts somewhat from the value of consolidation and may result in the issuance of separate invoices for distinct segments of the list.

Prepayment plans are offered by all major periodicals suppliers. The terms vary, but in general, a stated percentage of the amount paid is given in credit. This percentage is usually higher the earlier one pays. For instance, paying the following year's renewal invoice by April 30 of the current year may entitle the library to several percentage points in credit. On a payment of $250,000, this would provide the library with several thousands of dollars. Somewhat later, but still early, payment may result in lesser, but still significant, credit. There is generally some flexibility in how the credit is issued (such as credit memo or check) and how it may be used (toward any invoice, new subscriptions, or optional services, for example), although there may be a minimum amount required for participation. Alternatively, a vendor may reduce the service charge on subscriptions rather than actually paying interest. This can result in eliminating the service charge entirely, and may even reduce the cost of the titles below list price. Each library must carefully evaluate prepayment plans available from its subscription agents in order to determine which is most advantageous.

Obviously, increased buying power for libraries is hard to fault, even though the vendor will certainly gain more interest on the money that it will return to the library in credit. The vendor will also know, when it is time to pay the publishers, that it has the money in hand without having to wonder whether impecunious or recalcitrant institutions will renege at the last minute.

The institution to which a library is attached may take a dim view of such advance payments. Payment prior to receipt of goods is seldom welcomed. The institution may adopt the view that it, not the library's periodicals supplier, should collect all those months of interest. Librarians in such situations must become forceful advocates for the advantages to the library, and therefore to the institution, of advance payments.

One should be aware, also, that such advance payments can cause confusion about the price of the titles in question, since the further in advance the billing is done, the less firm the prices will be. Adjustments up or down will be made at a later date, but the manipulation of these data for fund accounting purposes, especially in automated systems, can be troublesome.

All sorts of customized products, whether invoices or management reports, exist and may be heavily depended upon by libraries. It is all expensive to the vendor and should be used with discretion. Customization that results in more efficient, accurate payment or that fits absolute institutional requirements is extremely valuable. Customized reports can provide useful data for use in budget projections and collection analysis, but uncritical acceptance of the bottom line of such reports can be dangerous. Since close examination is very time-consuming, the temptation is to concentrate on the grand totals. But only close examination can reveal errors either of data or of concept.

Another service that is widely touted, and into the development of which numerous vendors have invested considerable sums of money, is tape loading of both bibliographic records and invoices. Invoice tape loading promises an annual renewal invoice that would be zapped into the library's automated system from magnetic tape. But tape loading does not simply happen.

First, the tape must contain an element that matches an element in the library's online order record. This means that the library must have an order record for each title and that it must inform the vendor of the matching element, usually the order number. Sometimes this can be effected through tape transfer; sometimes manual input is required. The vendor must input all of these before the tape can be generated. If the library moves to another automated system, the process is likely to be repeated.

There are also costs involved in the actual tape load: computer time, staff time in loading and dealing with tape problems, paper for reports, staff time, and postage for returning used tapes to vendors. These might be brushed aside as minimal, but consider this: in order for the University at Albany Libraries, chronically short of staff, to tape load an annual renewal invoice for 4,058 titles, a project was organized in which approximately 1,000 hours of staff time were expended in the creation of online records and resolution of attendant problems. This resulted in cleaner files as well and was undeniably beneficial overall, but the project was a burden that lasted for months.

This was merely in preparation for the tape load, which, when finally accomplished, developed problems—as did the second annual renewal. For example, when the vendor exceeded the per-invoice line limit, the library's software froze the invoice. Lines beyond the limit could not be updated or corrected, nor could the invoice be balanced or given final authorization. Only the library programmer's ingenuity and system downtime overcame the problem. Over 600 potential problems were identified by the tape load warning report, which pinpoints such things as missing order numbers and prices. While invoices were being authorized online, further problems were identified. Over 160 hours of staff time went into resolving these problems before the invoices could be sent on for payment.

Yet, tape loading annual renewal invoices from this and other vendors is desirable in this library for several reasons: commitment to an online system with one source, a computer terminal, for all data; immediate online availability of price data; and computer-identified problems that result in greater, not less, scrutiny of the invoice by higher level staff. The end result is a higher degree of accuracy and broader access to information—and an opportunity for the library to demonstrate meticulous use of the materials budget. Although these gains have resulted from considerable effort by the staff of this library—not as a gift from the agent—there are considerable costs to the agent as well: development of the interface, provision of the tapes, and staff time in inputting linking data. It is important to keep in perspective the relative costs and contributions of subscription agents, system vendors, and libraries in improving these products. All such services must be critically evaluated in light of each library's goals.

Librarians eagerly anticipate price studies and projections by major periodicals suppliers and compare vendor's figures. It is important to remember, though, that projections of percentage price increases are fallible. The only true data for a library comes from its own files. Its unique title mix will determine how much the prices it pays will increase. This may be far different from anyone else's "average increase." Nevertheless, many libraries cannot compile their own figures and must rely on vendor data. Although it may be useful when the library makes its case for increased funding, the librarian must realize that such data are unreliable.

The array of specialized fee-based services offered by periodicals suppliers can be overwhelming. They can provide automation where the library's own institution cannot. They are generally mature and sophisticated systems continually upgraded to better answer customer demands.

Nevertheless, they should be considered with care. In some libraries, such services are paid from the materials budget, reducing monies available for acquistions. Useful though they may be, these electronic services can tie the library ever more securely to one vendor, increasing its profits and reducing competition.

New services are being offered all the time. Additions such as out-of-print lists and other specialized databases available for a fee are designed to make money for the company, whatever service they may provide to the library community. Remember, periodicals vendors sell *only* service; they do not touch the periodical issues themselves. The more services they can sell, the more successful they will be. The value of these services to any given library must be carefully weighed.

Service Charges

Most librarians pay far too little attention to service charges, how they are computed, and what they buy. Lists are moved between vendors and incentives blindly accepted, all in the name of a lower service charge. One of the more disturbing "promises" made in this area is put in the following terms: if library A moves certain titles from vendor Y to vendor Z, the library's service charge will decrease. Titles that are sought in this way are generally free of service charge from other vendors. They are desirable because they are profitable. If the titles to be moved carry no service charge themselves, the *percentage* of the total bill represented by the service charge will clearly decrease. The dollar amount paid in service charge may decrease as well if these zero service charge titles are numerous enough and discounted sufficiently to reduce some of the service charges on other titles. Precisely, what will happen is difficult to ascertain in advance. One must also consider what the loss of the titles will do to the list they are moved from.

It is also critical to look at the prices of the titles in question, not only at service charge. Foreign titles especially will not cost the same from all vendors. What has been gained if service charge is reduced but higher subscription prices are paid for the periodicals themselves? Focusing on the percent of the total bill represented by the service charge is misleading.

Another area of confusion is the fixed percentage service charge versus a variable rate. Which is best? Some agents make life simpler for everyone by charging a fixed percentage, say four percent, on all titles to all customers. Others give options. Does the library want a fixed or variable rate, and how should it be shown on the invoice? If tapes are loaded into an online system, how will the service charge work in the system? To answer these questions, it is useful to have some knowledge of how the vendors compute service charges.

The cost of a title to the vendor determines what the vendor charges the library for that title, but somewhere in the equation the vendor must account for other costs (e.g., inflation and overhead) and make a profit. If a publisher supplies a title to a vendor at a substantial discount, the vendor will be able to provide it to libraries without service charge. If a library were to have a list composed only of titles such as these, it could obtain its entire list free of service charge. The vendor's profit would come from the difference between the price it paid the publisher and the price it charged the customer. If a publisher supplies a title at a discount to one vendor, it will do so to all, but not necessarily at the same rate. All vendors covet subscriptions to such titles because they are profitable and they are good pubic relations.

Conversely, a list consisting solely of titles that are not discounted to the vendor would carry a high service charge. Thus, it is clear that the mixture of titles on a list is the critical factor in determining the service charge for that list. In general, science, technology, medical, and certain foreign titles (on a North-American supplied list) will help reduce the effect of service charges for social sciences and humanities titles.

Use of a fixed rate that is not the same for all customers, but is based on the individual library's title mix, tends to focus attention on the percentage rather than on the true cost and to be misleading.

As noted above, the percentage will decrease if the list is augmented by the addition of zero service charge titles, and three or four percent looks much better than six or eight percent, but what matters foremost is the actual price of the titles. If prices are high because the vendor's price structure is high or exchange rates are unfavorable, they will more than make up for a couple of percentage points in the service charge. For this reason, the University at Albany library has never accepted a fixed percentage service charge and has recently asked to have service charges shown line by line on the invoice.

Incentives are sometimes offered to gain a library as a customer or to get a library to augment its list. A vendor might offer incentives if the library moves certain titles to it or even if it refrains from moving titles away! This might take the form of free use of a service that normally carries a charge, at least for a period of time. An entire list might be gained in this manner, if the incentive is great enough. Service charges can also be set at a specified percentage for a given period of time, giving the library the security of knowing that the percentage will not rise. Surely, though, the prices will rise, and therefore the dollar amount paid in service charge will also increase. Moreover, this kind of agreement guarantees that the service charge will not go down. The most important price factor is cost per title. To avoid selecting offers with hidden pitfalls, some libraries expressly will not consider these offers directed at gaining immediate sales from specific libraries. They choose only from offers publicized widely and available to all customers. This a wise course.

Narrowing the Field

There are two ways to approach the process of narrowing the field. Having collected extensive data from several potential subscription agents, the library can judge which vendor comes closest to offering the services it needs at the best overall price. This allows a library to forego unneeded services and use an agent that both offers less and charges less.

A more aggressive approach to narrowing the field is the practice of pricing services individually so that libraries can select only those it needs. This practice is called "unbundling"—that is, breaking out individual services and attaching a price tag to each. This approach can be library driven, in which case a library negotiates with the vendor a price for its list and the services it requires. It can also be vendor driven in a "supermarket" approach, where customers take from vendors' shelves only those prepriced items they need.

The potential for realizing significant savings, especially as service charges rise, makes unbundling an attractive idea. Nevertheless, unbundling is not a magic wand. Some services will lend themselves to unbundling better than others, and entering into the process requires considerable knowledge on the part of librarians. There are also problems, such as in determining actual costs of individual services and questions revolving around how such unbundling would function in practice. It might be worthwhile for subscription agents to offer discounts for "good behavior" by the library, which would reduce vendor costs by, for example, prompt and accurate claiming on the part of the library. Unbundling would add a level of complexity and make demands on librarians that do not exist in a bundled environment. And, again, this focus on service charge can divert one from examining the actual price of the materials being purchased.

As with books, one must consider North American versus foreign vendors. The country-of-origin theory applies to serials for the same reasons: better understanding of local markets and advantageous pricing, although the latter is less noticeable when the U.S. dollar is weak.

There is no justification for purchasing all of one's titles from one supplier unless the list is small, highly specialized, or the library has solid data indicating that total costs (not just service charges) will be lower and service will be superior.

North American subscription agents may list third world publications in their catalogs, but may not supply them as successfully as a vendor in the country of publication. It is worthwhile to develop relationships with foreign vendors, as described in the previous chapter, and to put extra effort into accommodating any special requests such as payment or acknowledgment of receipt of issues.

CONTINUATIONS

VENDOR OR PUBLISHER?

Serials that are not periodicals on subscription are often referred to as "continuations" or "standing orders." This group may include annuals, irregular serials, monographic series, and the like. As a rule they are not billed in advance, although certain exceptional items such as *Beilstein's Handbuch der Organischen Chemie* may be. Usually, they are shipped and billed as published.

Consolidating continuation orders is done for the same reasons as for periodicals, but the methods of billing, vendor strengths and problems encountered are somewhat different.

As with other types of material, some publishers may require direct orders or may offer incentives for ordering direct and they should be considered. It can happen, over a period of years, that standing orders for a number of titles from a given publisher are placed with various suppliers. Perhaps two vendors supply several each and a few more are coming direct from the publisher. The publisher may develop an incentive program to encourage placement of orders directly with it. Examination of invoices will show any discounts given or service charges applied. Crucial, of course, is service. Has one of the vendors needed constant claims in order to supply the material? What is the publisher's record? Does the publisher provide a specific customer service representative? Do phone calls to this person inspire confidence? Comparisons can be made and some conclusion drawn about the value of consolidating the orders with the publisher. Certain types of serials are generally obtained direct from the publisher: microform serials, services, city directories, U.S. government publications, and very expensive titles such as *Biological Abstracts*.

In order to be successful at supplying continuations, a vendor must maintain a separate operation. Personnel must understand serials, and files must accommodate their often unpredictable nature. Libraries may have special requests, such as wishing to receive every other year of an annual, so this possibility must be built into the system. Some serials, such as conference proceedings, move from one publisher to another, making a standing order almost impossible to maintain. Monographic series are another problem area: they too sometimes change publisher, and they may publish no new volumes for long intervals and then publish several in one year. Their irregularity makes allocating funds for them difficult, and provokes the question of whether standing orders are justified at all. Numbered monographic series may be one of the few instances of publishers understanding the library market. Who else would feel compelled to purchase every number of a monographic series? This practice often results in unexamined material entering library collections. Such series have been known to include books only remotely relating to the series title or to be no more than repackaged reprints. Moreover, monographs supplied on standing order are not discounted. The ongoing nature of these materials, coupled with their frequent lack of regularity, makes them particularly challenging. A vendor that can start new standing orders promptly, report with clarity and dependability, and supply a wide range of serial publications well, will succeed in meeting the library's needs.

The same kind of careful winnowing process that goes into the selection of vendors for periodicals must apply to the selection of vendors for other serials. Prices, services, and the quality of service will vary widely among vendors. The multitude of automated services developed by periodicals vendors does not exist for other serials because they do not lend themselves as well to them. Nevertheless, customized management reports and the like are available, and vendor files themselves are automated, resulting in better tracking and reporting. Service charges as such do not exist. Some discounts may occur; some items will be sent as "net"; and some will carry individual service charges.

A careful selection process must take place. One cannot assume that because a given vendor is fully satisfactory for books it will necessarily be the choice for continuations. There must be a balance between price and ability to supply the material successfully. Whereas a library might go for high discount on single-item orders of trade books, it might choose to pay more for continuations from a vendor that services them well. Price considerations may be less critical than for books, while special services may be less important than for periodicals, making continuations a hybrid of sorts between books and periodicals.

MAKING THE CHOICE

There is no substitute for knowledge of one's own goals combined with critical evaluation of potential vendors. Service and price are the bottom line, and each librarian must make an educated but subjective evaluation of whether a prospective supplier will be able to provide what is needed and at the best price. If a library prefers the bare bones approach, it is best to choose a supplier that will provide the essentials at a minimal service charge.

Another important consideration is how the vendor will suit the library as a partner. This is important, given the intense, long-term nature of the relationship. If a library has an extensive periodicals list in engineering, for instance, a library with a similar emphasis should be consulted. Discuss specific problem titles with both

SUMMARY

To establish a viable partnership with a serials supplier:

1. Know institutional policies and objectives.
2. Consider the advantages and disadvantages of using a vendor or ordering direct from the publisher.
3. Evaluate vendor prices, services, and service charges.
4. Decide how many vendors to use and which vendors.
5. Communicate.
6. Evaluate.

libraries and vendors. Exactly how are problems dealt with? What pleased or displeased other libraries?

There is also the question of how many vendors to use. Some kind of list splitting seems advisable in all but the smallest libraries. At the University at Albany Libraries, the preference is to deal with a relatively small group of vendors each supplying a fairly substantial list of those titles it services best. We find that country-of-origin vendors provide advantageous pricing and service. We use a number of third world suppliers for serials published in their countries and place a certain number of direct orders as well. Moreover, since each major vendor offers desired services such as invoice tape loading, and since our own system provides the reports we need, consolidation with *one* vendor is not attractive.

5 BECOMING PARTNERS

Once a choice has been made, one's work has just begun. In order to achieve an effective and mutually beneficial partnership, the relationship must be fostered and monitored with care. Before sending a batch of orders to a new vendor, an account should be set up through initial contact with the company, with library and vendor requirements set forth.

When a decision is made to use a particular vendor, that vendor will probably request that a customer profile be prepared for its files. This specifies such things as format of invoices, reporting period and format, cancellation date, and the like. For subscriptions, the vendor will want to know whether a common expiration date is desired, whether to renew for multiple years, how the service charge is to be handled, and whether invoice tape loading is expected. Likewise, the library must know and understand the vendor's policies—and be sure all appropriate library staff members are aware of what the library has requested of the vendor. One can hardly fault a vendor for not reporting monthly if quarterly reports were specified!

ORDERS

It is in the library's interest to supply the fullest, clearest, most accurate ordering information possible. If a library sends out an ambiguous order and does not get what it wants, it should not blame the vendor. Orders should be submitted in whatever format the vendor requests, although institutional realities may come into play as well. For instance, a library's degree of automation significantly affects the ordering process, as does the particular automated system in use. Some libraries must or prefer to print and mail orders showing full bibliographic information, while others are content to transmit ISBN numbers alone electronically. It is worthwhile for a library to explore with vendors the format and content of its order forms to determine whether the form itself may cause difficulty for the vendor and therefore delay obtaining desired material. The envelope should be clearly and correctly addressed.

For subscriptions, the library's account number should be specified. Essential bibliographic data should be supplied, as well as a clearly stated starting point (volume and issue number, date). If the vendor uses title numbers, they should be shown. If the library has special requests, they must be clearly stated.

Sound too simple? Consider ordering from the vendors' viewpoint. They receive thousands of orders in various formats, with information variously arranged. Moreover, the orderer (library) demands a variety of special conditions regarding such elements as shipping, reporting, and invoicing. Compare this to other business transactions, in which the supplier provides the order form and inventory number and spells out shipping and billing mechanisms. Instead, the library uses the ISBN, on which vendors rely heavily. However, incorrect ISBNs are not rare and can easily cause the vendor to obtain the wrong book from the publisher. Only careful manual checking will prevent the book from being shipped to the library. Incomplete and incorrect orders not only fail to get the library what it needs, they cost vendors money, which can be recovered only through general pricing structures for all customers.

Minimal order verification on the part of the library results in extra work and expense for the library in duplicates and wrong books, as well as extra work and expense for the vendor in verifying, correcting, or even rejecting an order. Libraries have the best tools for bibliographic verification in OCLC and RLIN. They are placing the order, and it is their job to do so accurately.

Most vendors are agreeable to special requests, but the totality of thousands of libraries and hundreds of variations in special requests is costly to implement. Perhaps because most vendors are accommodating, libraries tend to take it for granted that special requests will be met. It is an interesting exercise to imagine being on the receiving end of all these special requests and to wonder whether they are really all necessary.

THE THIRD PARTNER

The publisher is the unseen third partner. Publishers' behavior has a great impact on vendors and, ultimately, on libraries. Vendors complain that publishers ignore claims, ship the wrong books, have arcane rules for ordering, change distributors, are unreliable, and have varied and unfair pricing and discount policies.

At the close of their fiscal years, vendors are often owed considerable sums by libraries. At the same time, they may be owed large sums by publishers for returned books. Vendors must endure difficulties with publishers because publishers are the source of their books. Although vendors put a great deal of effort into publisher relations, ultimately it is the publisher who controls the game.

RUSH ORDERS

Similarly, it is wise to clarify expectations for "rush" orders. What does the library mean by "rush"? What does the vendor do differently when it receives such an order? Are these books shipped differently? Is the library willing to pay a premium for rapid delivery? On foreign orders in particular, shipping by air is essential if "rush" is to have much meaning. Does the vendor automatically do this, or must it be specified on each rush order? How much will it cost? If a library is serious about rush requests, it should track various vendors' performance on rush material separately from regular orders. If a rush is a problem for books, it is meaningless for subscriptions. A few days gained through rapid handling by the vendor hardly matters when it takes six to eight weeks to start a North American subscription.

REPORTS

All book vendors provide reports on open orders. Vendors' reports differ from each other in frequency and format, and in many cases the library has some choices. When making selections, the library must consider its own capacity to process vendor reports. Given the library's files, whether automated or manual, what is the most efficient format and order in which to receive reports? Will there be sufficient staff to process reports quickly after they are received? Staff assigned this task must be sufficiently knowledgeable to question suspect reports. It is essential that reports received from vendors be treated seriously and their messages quickly assimilated into the order record. Obviously, this is more easily done in automated systems than manual files, but it must be done nevertheless. A well-documented order history will go a long way toward mollifying unhappy selectors or patrons who need a book not yet received.

Orders for periodicals may elicit confirmation from the vendor as well as reports on delayed publications or queries. For instance, if the library specified the subscription to begin with Volume 10, 1991, but, in fact, Volume 9 will be issued in 1991, the vendor will want to know whether the library wants Volume 9. Questions of this nature should be answered promptly. In addition to ongoing queries and reports, the vendor may send an extensive report with the annual renewal invoice. For a large list, this can be a formidable document, filled with messages about title changes, discontinued or suspended publications, delayed publications, frequency changes, availability of indexes, and the like.

The library has an obligation to record and act upon this information as each situation demands. Not to do so will only result in increased and unnecessary work later for both library and vendor.

CLAIMS

Claims for material not received cause considerable work for both library staff and vendors. This is another reason for rapid processing of vendor reports. It is readily apparent when examining records whether the vendor has recently reported on the item. If so, a claim can be avoided. Claims should be kept to a minimum to limit the burden on the staffs of both library and vendor. This is why automated systems that produce automatic claims have caused consternation on the receiving end. Claiming should not be foregone on the assumption that vendor reports will cover everything, but careful use of vendor reports will greatly facilitate the claiming process.

The claim form itself should be clear and readily distinguishable from an order form. It should provide a place for the vendor's response, boxes to check for various conditions (e.g., out of stock, out of print, date shipped), as well as space for longer answers. The library should expect responses to its claims, and most vendors will do so. Publishers generally are less accommodating, and it is not uncommon for repeated claims to go unanswered. Much staff time can then go into telephone calls, fax messages, and the like in an attempt to obtain material that was ordered and very likely has funds encumbered for it.

Claiming missed issues of periodicals is a far larger task than claiming slow or incomplete shipment of book orders. Serials librarians are inclined to feel that vendors do not respond quickly enough to claims and do not follow up unless prodded by the library. They may feel that they might as well prod the publisher directly. Some libraries do so and are pleased with the results. Agents may feel at the mercy of publishers' claims policies, refusal to acknowledge claims, poor distribution policies, or failure to print sufficient copies. At the same time, they are being dunned by irate librarians who have gaps in their collections. Nor are vendors unaware of the problems librarians cause—errors, premature claiming, late claiming, moving subscriptions from one vendor to another, idiosyncratic local requirements, late renewals, and the like.

Claims must be promptly and accurately processed. Many publishers of periodicals refuse to honor claims after a period of weeks. They also complain that it is mainly libraries that fail to receive their periodicals and that, therefore, it is their own fault through misdirected mail, failure to note variations such as frequency and title changes, and incorrect check-in. While this complaint is not entirely unjustified, careful adherence to procedures can reduce the number of superfluous claims.

RETURNS

Returning books is an expensive and annoying task for both library and vendor. Nevertheless, all reputable vendors accept returns. Some will even accept returns for reasons other than their own error or defective books. Sometimes they accept books that publishers will not take back, absorbing the cost. Inexpensive books, however, are not worth returning; some libraries pay for and discard rather than return them. Careful records must be kept on returned items in case the vendor fails to respond or asserts that the returned book was never received. In that case, the transaction must be tracked in order to assure the desired result (i.e., replacement copy, different book, or credit memo).

It is inevitable that some serial material will have to be returned as well—the result of duplicate subscriptions or the wrong item sent on standing order. As with book returns, advance communication with the vendor is important, and return instructions should be followed to the letter, supplemented by good documentation at the library's end.

CANCELLATIONS

Vendors should take cancellations, for any reason, with good grace, and most do. Nevertheless, the vendor will have invested some expense in the processing of an order that ultimately comes to nothing, and the loss of a subscription or standing order can mean significantly reduced business. In fairness to the vendor and to minimize its own problems, the library should cancel with as much advance warning as possible. Some book orders cannot be cancelled. Once the vendor obtains the book from the publisher, the publisher will not take it back. If the library will not buy it, the vendor is left with the book and its cost. All good vendors report such situations before shipping the book.

When a library affirms its intention to accept books under these circumstances, it must record the decision and should never try to renege. Cancelling periodicals in mid-subscription should be avoided because publishers frequently refuse mid-subscription cancellations. Cancelling should take the form of simply asking the vendor not to renew for the next cycle.

A standing order will remain active in the vendor's file until either the vendor or the library cancels it. A standing order may show no receipts for years, but technically still be in existence. When something is published after a lengthy hiatus, the library is obligated to accept the material, even if it now wishes to cancel. It cannot return the shipment and cancel simultaneously. It can keep the shipment and immediately cancel to prevent future shipments, but it is far better to cancel unwanted titles as part of regular review of ongoing commitments.

ERRORS

Vendors, like librarians, make mistakes. The wrong book, the wrong edition, or the wrong number of copies may be shipped. Shipping may be charged where a contract prohibits doing so, or discount may differ from that stated in a contract. Items may be duplicated in error. Monographs in series may be duplicated between approval plan and standing order. A book may be supplied on a standing order for another title. A standing order set up to be supplied in alternate years may be supplied in consecutive years. Subscriptions may be billed even after confirmation of cancellation.

Careful receiving procedures are needed to intercept errors before books are property stamped or otherwise defaced, although a good vendor should accept returns of stamped books in the case of its own error. Errors should be dealt with promptly and the problem communicated clearly but without rancor to the vendor. Data should be kept so that a vendor's error rate can be determined. If a vendor's rate of errors becomes unacceptable, stronger measures will be needed, including the possibility of dropping that vendor entirely. Along the way, maintain frequent communication and give the vendor every opportunity to improve its performance. Once a vendor falls from grace, however, it is often difficult for librarians to accept that vendor again. There are just too many other vendors eager for the business and too little time to waste on one that is below par.

PAYMENT

Ultimately, payment is what business is all about. Reputable vendors do not demand advance payment, although small publishers and dealers not focused on the library market often do. A library vendor will make such prepayments for the library, usually for a small service charge and often with the stipulation that the material is nonreturnable. However, this is a small price for the library to pay to avoid the inconvenience and possible loss of funds represented by advance payment. Some libraries are prohibited from making advance payments, or they may lack any way of obtaining a check quickly, or they may require an invoice before payment can be made. Conditions such as these are easily overcome by letting a vendor act as go-between.

Be sure to understand fully each vendor's policy regarding service charges, what the service charge buys for the library, and what the alternatives are. Of course, most vendors also offer discounts. Understanding this side of the vendor's fees is also essential.

INVOICES

Librarians should scrutinize invoices to ascertain whether the expected discount was in fact given. The invoice itself is an important document. Major vendors will format their invoices as the library wishes, within certain parameters. Items can be listed in whatever order is desired. Order numbers can be printed as desired, lines skipped between items, and a specific number of copies of the invoice provided. The invoice can be packed with the shipment or mailed separately. Billing can be in a specified currency. Clarity is essential and will save both vendor and library time and money.

Checking the accuracy of invoices is also important in vendor evaluation. Everything from order numbers to charges should be verified. The accuracy of the order number is especially important if it serves as the link in an automated fund accounting system.

Vendors should be told of, and are generally tolerant of, ways in which payment may be controlled by the institutions libraries belong to. Foreign vendors may have to accept payment in U.S. dollars rather than their own currencies. All major foreign vendors serving the U.S. market accept this situation, many having U.S. bank accounts to which payment can be sent. Some institutions, as a matter of policy, do not send a copy of the invoice with the check even though virtually every vendor requests it. Likewise, the length of time it takes for payment to reach the vendor may be partly beyond the librarian's control because of bureaucratic requirements. A large vendor is generally tolerant of these vagaries, but a small publisher or a learned society may be less so.

COMMUNICATION

An underlying assumption behind this discussion is that lines of communication between vendor and library are kept open. Vendors need to hear from their customers and libraries can greatly influence vendors if they choose to do so. The development of a partnership between libraries and vendors has been largely the result of a greater understanding of libraries by vendors. They have grasped the diversity among their customers and developed flexible systems in an attempt to keep them happy. The fact, for example, that more and more vendors employ librarians as sales representatives and in other capacities has greatly increased communication. Librarians appear to have been slower to become educated about vendors.

It is useful for librarians to put into writing descriptions of ongoing problems and the ways in which they should be resolved. Likewise, they should send written compliments to a company or a particular employee (and his supervisor) when something is done extraordinarily well.

A customer representative who knows the library's account and with whom library staff can develop a good working relationship is a great boon to the library and to the vendor. In facilitating the order process, in providing accurate, cordial, prompt service, these people gain the vendor untold good will and increased business. Most acquisitions librarians can name specific customer service representatives who are memorable for the quality of service they provide. They are to be cultivated and complimented.

The sales representative is also a valuable person, from whom much can be learned. And the librarian should openly communicate to the sales rep the good and bad about the vendor. They should neither be refused appointment without strong reason nor viewed as sources of free lunches. When a crisis occurs, having the sales rep on one's side can be helpful indeed.

Communication is the glue that holds the librarian/vendor partnership together—not just discussion of problems, but working together to influence the future form of information services. Such a partnership presupposes that the acquisitions librarian be informed and active. He or she needs to understand publishing and the role of the vendor, as well as developments that affect the information industry. There is no substitute for reading about the issues discussed in the professional literature, participating in forums and committees of the American Library Association and other professional associations, and simply discussing the issues with other professionals.

AUTOMATION

Automation offers hope for resolution of at least some of these problems. The promise of X-12 is standardization across and beyond the publishing world; the linkage of publisher, vendor, and library systems; the virtual elimination of duplicative input; and

SUMMARY

To make the partnership work:

1. Consider the vendor's point of view.
2. Maintain standards of accuracy and timeliness.
3. Select vendors with care.
4. Evaluate.
5. Communicate.

communication computer to computer. Add to that the possibility of scanning a barcode to initiate an order, and much opportunity for error disappears.

Existing automation at both the library end and the vendor end is a major factor in the library/vendor relationship. Automation has been the driving force behind much of the recent proliferation in vendor services. A library without an automated acquisitions system can use a vendor's customized invoices and computer-produced management reports. A library that does have an automated acquisitions system can load vendor information directly into its system. Various reports and checks for duplicate records can be done at the time of tape load.

6 CONTRACTS AND BIDDING

Some states and the federal government, in the interest of ensuring fair and cost-effective use of taxpayers' money, attempt to regulate the purchase of library materials, along with the procurement of everything else state or federal agencies might need. Libraries—including school, college, and university libraries, as well as libraries of state agencies, military institutions, and the like—are compelled to follow rules that have little applicability to library purchasing.

After some educatory work on the part of librarians, legislation requiring library materials to be purchased on contract or through bid may be rescinded or libraries exempted or regulations changed. But memories are short, and some years later new laws may again come into force that wreak havoc on the acquisitions process. The legislators and bureaucrats who make and enforce the regulations seldom have any knowledge of library operations. They may not even realize that libraries are covered by procurement regulations. When this is brought to their attention, they may not always understand why the purchase of books and periodicals is any different from the purchase of pencils, automobiles, or letterhead.

THE BOOK CONTRACT

One common form of bureaucratic control of purchasing is the requirement that purchases be made only from a vendor under contract. There are numerous variations on this theme.

Until recently, New York State had one of the more rational and least troublesome contract situations, while Texas had one of the worst. The New York State Book Contract is a document that is issued at several year intervals. On it are listed a great many book dealers (currently 46), along with the terms under which they sell various types of material. State requirements are spelled out in detail, and the scope of the contract is clearly limited to in-print North American monographs.

This situation came about through the concerted efforts of librarians and vendors, who about nine years ago made their case known and understood. Prior book contracts had been highly restrictive, listing only a few vendors. Expanding the list made it possible for any library bound by the contract to find on it a suitable vendor. Because vendors on this contract offer varying discounts and other terms, each library can exercise its own judgment regarding price and service.

This type of open-ended statewide contract limited to North American monographs does not seriously hamper library activities, particularly because it recognizes the existence of sole sources and permits going off contract in such cases. It does mean, however, that acquisitions librarians must know the book contract thoroughly and be aware of changes in regulations that may affect library operations.

At the other end of the spectrum is Texas, where one vendor has been under contract to provide books and AV materials to all state-affiliated libraries. The situation in this state improved somewhat in 1983, when certain materials, including foreign items, were exempted from the bidding process.

The case against statewide contracts was made superbly 15 years ago by Calvin Boyer in an article that analyzed information from 50 state-supported academic libraries, directors of 45 state purchasing agencies, and ten library vendors. His overwhelming and carefully documented conclusion was that:

1. Unmistakable evidence demonstrates that statewide contracts are a disservice to the principal parties involved—the state, the library, and the vendor.
2. Typically, libraries bound by such contracts are forced to spend precious staff time and portions of limited budgets when faced with a change of contractors and/or inadequate service from the vendor.
3. In summation, the state and its state-supported academic libraries can be better served by allowing each individual library to select the optimum method of meeting its own unique set of needs.

This article should be read and kept at hand by acquisitions librarians in state-affiliated libraries and should be provided to legislators and bureaucrats should the need arise. Librarians in state-affiliated libraries must be knowledgeable and prepared to make their cases.

BIDDING

"Putting out for bid" is a dreaded phrase among acquisitions librarians. Those who work for agencies where purchase of most anything is preceded by a lengthy process of obtaining bids knows that even for non-library materials it is a flawed system. Cheap is frequently just that—cheap—and it often results in pens that will not write and correction fluid that does not cover ink. The hidden costs in staff time and stop-gap measures are incalculable.

When it comes to library materials, bidding is even more disastrous. Not only may libraries get cheap, they may get nothing. And the collections will show the gaps forever.

Daniel Melcher, in *Melcher on Acquisition* (Bowker), offers an excellent precis of the inapplicability of bidding to library materials. He concludes:

> There is danger in letting any large contract swing completely from one supplier to another between one year and the next. A supplier who has been giving satisfaction ought not to be dumped completely just because another bidder who is an unknown quantity comes along and bids a shade lower. Such an all-or-nothing competition means in effect that only giants—or fools—can even compete.

When periodicals lists are put out for bid, and the bid is won by a vendor other than the one currently in use, libraries face inordinate demands on staff time as records for each title must be changed to reflect the new vendor. In addition, while staff time is diverted to this task, current check-in may fall behind. Moreover, switched subscriptions frequently are plagued by missed issues and payment problems in the changeover process. It is then up to the library to rectify a situation that could easily have been avoided. Worst of all, the new vendor may provide below-par services. Ultimately, the library's clientele suffers because needed information is not available and uncounted money is wasted in wages for library staff dealing with problems.

Examples of the negative effects of bidding for library materials abound. In 1972 school and public libraries in Hawaii found themselves unable to purchase books for over six months due to contract difficulties. When the contract was split between two vendors, one contested it. This vendor was opposed by librarians in any case due to their dissatisfaction with its performance in the past. The months of haggling did not end even when the contract was finally awarded (split between the non-contesting vendor and a third one, leaving the contester out). Left to their own devices, the libraries could have supplied new books to their patrons throughout the year and the state could have been spared the expense of the entire process.

Recently, New York State has required putting out for bid through a mechanism called the New York State Contract Reporter such things as membership in the Center for Research Libraries and sole-source publications where the aggregate price of several standing order renewals exceeds $20,000 within a 60-day period. Meanwhile, the supplier believes that a valid standing order exists and expects payment. Eventually, he will get it, but not until considerable time has elapsed.

The damaging effects of the mentality that, unfamiliar with libraries, books, and research, believes "a book is a book is a book" is shown in the following example: An item desired for the rare book collection is found in a dealer's catalog. The librarian calls the dealer and asks that the item be held, pending the confirming purchase order. The librarian prepares the order, and passes it through the campus purchasing office, which puts it out for bid. A low bid is received from another vendor and the book supplied. However, it is a cheap reprint, not the desired item. In the meantime, the rare book dealer, tired of waiting, has sold the item elsewhere.

Some vendors obtain contracts by bidding very high discounts. In fact, they may return many orders as "out of print," although these are merely those titles the vendor does not wish to supply at the stated discount rate. The library must then prove that the book can be obtained elsewhere before eventually being allowed to pursue the order.

Sometimes vendors who have high discounts will artificially inflate the list price of the book before applying the discount. This is very difficult to prove because list prices can be very fluid. All of this points up the failure of the contract/bidding system as far as libraries are concerned.

VENDOR OPINION

Needless to say, reputable vendors do not engage in such tactics. In most instances, vendors want the same things librarians want, plus the opportunity to make a fair profit. When it comes to the contract and bidding process, vendors are no more enthusiastic than librarians. This was made clear in response to a questionnaire soliciting vendor comments on bidding and contracts. The questionnaire was sent to well-known, widely used vendors of various sizes. Only two were foreign-based companies. Vendors of both books and serials were included.

Five of the eight who responded characterized the expenses involved in doing business with libraries covered by state book contracts as moderate to sizable. In order to recover this expense, three reduce the discount offered, while one increases the service charge. Another tries to be selective in submitting bids in order to control costs. One mentioned reducing discounts across the board to all customers, not only to libraries covered by contracts.

Five of the eight said that bidding had never caused them to offer services or pricing structures that would not have been offered otherwise. One said that less is offered in a bid situation. When asked why they participate in contracts and submit bids, vendors felt they had no choice if they wanted to remain in the field.

Regarding possible benefits of the contract/bid system, the vendors were unanimously negative. All eight said they suffered from participation, while only two noted, in addition, some gain in business as a benefit. Five felt the large vendors were the most likely to benefit; one said none would benefit; and one (a large vendor) believes a smaller vendor would benefit. Comments included such phrases as: "everybody loses"; it is a "restrictive and costly process with no significant gain in business"; "it impedes competition"; and "libraries get no better and possibly worse discount than they could negotiate themselves."

An invitation to comment at the end of the questionnaire resulted in some remarkable responses. Lengthy essays and copies of articles were sent. Comments were unanimously negative. Vendors not only cited such problems as increased costs and loss of business but also focused on problems faced by the libraries involved. They recognized the denial of the librarian's prerogative to choose, the increased workload imposed by the bid process, the costs to a library of switching subscriptions, and the costs of poor service if a contract is awarded on price alone. One pointed out that critical elements such as professionalism, integrity, and flexibility are not part of the bid process.

WHAT CAN BE DONE?

Librarians can and must take action to help rectify this intolerable situation. First, the acquisitions librarian must be thoroughly informed about the requirements of the state that apply to library purchases. Go to the source. Is this a law or an administrative regulation? Obtain copies of the law(s) and/or regulation(s) and understand them. Know the avenues for effecting change. Get to know people in the local purchasing office, particularly its head and/or the person who oversees library purchases. Treat these people with respect and attempt to educate them in the idiosyncrasies of library purchasing. Never adopt a negative attitude. If operating in a contract environment, know the contract inside and out, particularly what it does not cover. If a bidding situation is unavoidable, the best course is the use of RFPs (Request for Proposal). A pure bid situation will be based solely on price, whereas an RFP can specify a host of requirements. It creates a competitive negotiation environment, which can ensure that the library will obtain what it needs. If you do not have experience in such matters, try to find a librarians who has already been through the process and can provide assistance. It may be possible to obtain copies of RFPs from other libraries, which can serve as models. Consult local purchasing officers in whom you have some confidence. Vendors who have been through the process with others will be happy to assist in developing language, but one must be aware of potential ethical and legal problems inherent in making such use of a potential bidder. There is no reason to "go it alone," even in the smallest library. Seeking the expertise that will assist the library in achieving its goals is well worth the effort.

It is best to know the market and be able to predict with some accuracy which vendors are likely to participate. One should also be prepared to monitor the situation as time passes and bids come in. Bids from inappropriate quarters may indicate the need for writing a tighter RFP. In some cases, the library can contest the selection of such a source by preparing thorough justification showing why the low bidder is unacceptable and another should be selected instead. Again, preparedness and perseverance are essential.

Many vendors have more experience with bids and contracts than do librarians. They can provide advice as bids are being developed and share general knowledge about the process. Vendors may also participate with librarians in attempts to change existing practice or bid structure. When the New York State Book Contract was broadened, vendors were active participants (along with librarians) in bringing about needed changes. Some still refer to that period as the time they spent "camped in Albany" pursuing what at times seemed like a hopeless goal, but the outcome was favorable for all concerned and well worth the effort. Likewise, when the development of contracts and the necessity of submitting

SUMMARY
To make the best of bids and contracts:

1. Avoid bid situations.
2. Get to know local purchasing officers.
3. Learn about local rules and regulations.
4. Write clear, detailed RFPs.
4. Monitor open bids.
5. Educate the bureaucracy about the failure of bidding as a means of obtaining library materials.

bids occurs, many vendors willingly participate despite the ill treatment and expense they incur.

Once a library and vendor are joined by contract, each can contribute to developing a positive partnership. If the contract has gone to the library's preferred vendor, such as its current periodicals supplier, both can breathe a sigh of relief and continue business as usual. If, on the other hand, the contract has gone to a vendor the library opposed and it must change subscriptions to a new provider, both the librarian and the vendor must put great effort into easing the transition. It is in the interests of both for the new vendor to receive complete and accurate information about existing subscriptions. Can the vendor help the library in compiling this information by providing on-site assistance? Librarians are rightly skeptical of promises of an accurate and trouble-free changeover of subscriptions. The vendor who accepts the financial rewards of receiving business through a contract and neglects to provide service that is at least on a par with what the library enjoyed before will reap much ill will. A vendor in this situation who surpasses the former vendor in service and assistance, who turns the library's anticipated nightmare into a pleasant experience, will gain a loyal customer. But, if the nightmare becomes reality, the library will harbor resentment toward the vendor and will leave for another at the first opportunity.

Purchase of materials is part of the librarian's professional responsibility. Therefore, no effort is too great in the attempt to obtain exemption for libraries from all contract and bidding requirements.

7 APPROVAL PLANS

ORIGINS

Although it is possible to trace the origin of the approval plan back a century and a half to an arrangement between the British Museum and an American bookseller, the approval plan as it is known today is a child of the twentieth-century post-World War II boom in economic development and education. Through the United States government's Farmington Plan, foreign booksellers collected books for American libraries, initiating the development of approval plans in North America and making certain foreign vendors an integral part of the North American library market. Large-scale approval plans were developed by the Richard Abel Company during the 1960s. Their creation reflects a time of academic library expansion, generous materials budgets, and low inflation rates. Libraries, particularly larger ones, found themselves unable to readily obtain the books they needed and increasingly turned to book jobbers to supply them. Although the jobbers filled an important role as intermediaries between publishers and libraries, they fell short as a means of obtaining single copies of a very broad spectrum of publications. There was simply too much to deal with on a one-to-one basis. Thus, Abel began on a large scale to gather books for libraries, based on their instructions as to what subjects, publishers, and formats should be included. The libraries were given the right to return unwanted items.

These plans were also called "gathering plans," a term more appropriate to the past than the present. At that time large libraries did indeed "gather" (all university press titles, all U.S. output, or all the output from specified countries within certain fairly simple parameters, for example), and collections grew magnificently. Libraries prided themselves not only on the size of their collections, but sometimes on the size of their uncataloged backlogs. Arranging with a vendor to supply in bulk was certainly easier than individually selecting each title. Soon other vendors began to offer approval plans. They developed various methods for profiling the library's needs and for selecting books to meet those needs. They could provide announcement slips in addition to or instead of books. Eventually, much of the process became computerized. Although initially there was some controversy about whether librarians were abdicating their collection development responsibilities and vendors were taking advantage of libraries, approval plans have remained a constant, especially in academic libraries.

APPROVAL PLANS TODAY

Today, a number of vendors, both North American and European, offer approval plans. Each vendor has put considerable effort into the development of its plan; they differ markedly. They are also more complex to maintain for both vendor and library than they once were. Gone are the days of "gathering" for all but a few libraries, and gone too is the very simple profile. The days of minimal scrutiny of the books sent on approval are also in the past.

Approval plans are still common in medium and large academic libraries, and there is some indication that smaller libraries are making increased use of them as well. Association of Research Libraries statistics for 1987 showed $25.8 million spent on North American and foreign approval plans among 81 libraries. There are, of course, pros and cons. For librarians, perhaps the primary advantage is the fact that they can save considerable staff time that would be spent on selecting and preparing individual orders for those books. The vendor's staff replaces the library's staff in certain ways. Moreover, a good plan from a dependable vendor will supply current books in a timely fashion, and the books will be supplied at an agreed-upon discount. In addition, fine-tuned, computerized profiling can serve general and specialized collections alike.

Assuming that an approval plan accurately reflects publishing output, it can have a levelling influence on book publishing in that it is a disinterested provider of books in the subject areas covered. This can balance the tendency of some faculty members or selectors to favor certain subjects or publishers. Of course, levelling of purchasing can also be enforced by strict allocation of funds and by a high level of professionalism on the part of selectors. It can also be obviated by injudicious acceptance and rejection of approval books.

MANAGEMENT CONSIDERATIONS

It can be difficult to predict and control the products of approval plans because they are automatically subject to variations in publisher output. Thus, budgeting for approval plans is imprecise. Expenditures can easily outstrip projections. In recent years, marked by budgetary limitations, rising costs, and a weak dollar, approval plans have been known to outstrip their budgets in the same way that serials have overrun theirs. In an emergency a plan can be turned off, but with resulting gaps in the collection. Cost considerations can impair the functioning of an approval plan. Arbitrary price limits, reduction of the publishers included, sudden cut-off of a plan—all prevent that plan from supplying the library with materials that should be in the collection.

One must avoid keeping marginal material just because it is in hand and must beware of over-dependence on approval plans. Even while making use of the vendors' services and staffs, a library must continue monitoring and augmenting the plan. Some libraries that have not used approval plans object to them on just this basis: that selection should not be turned over to a vendor. Nevertheless, approval plans can be extremely useful.

Accidental duplication, while never desirable, is especially frowned upon in times of budgetary stringency. Aided by automation, vendors have developed ways to avoid duplicating firm-orders and standing order titles, but library staff members must remain alert to intercept duplication before books have been defaced. Books that once flowed unimpeded into library collections are now more often examined individually by selectors and individually accepted or rejected. They are sometimes rejected on the basis of price alone, a practice once unheard of. Selectors have an ongoing role to play in the maintenance of approval plans that goes far beyond their original establishment.

Likewise, members of the acquisitions department may actively manage the plans, monitoring adherence to profile by the vendor, screening out duplication, and providing information to selectors about previous editions or volumes held. They must understand collection development goals, vendor operations, local fiscal constraints, and the publishing industry. They must keep data on how well the plan is working, delivery times, pricing, and returns. They must also manage the processing of the books and their payment, which will likely differ from other routines in the department. The actual receipt of the books in acquisitions will likely vary from the receipt of a firm-order and will therefore require special procedures. Bibliographic records may be tape loaded into an online system, making the records available before the books arrive. A report may then be generated, pointing to possible duplication or other problems. Knowledgeable staff members are needed to deal with such problems.

Books will be shipped regularly—and shipments may be large, numbering hundreds of books. There may be more than one plan supplying large numbers of books. These shipments must be managed to maintain an orderly flow of books through the record creation, review, receiving, and payment process, recognizing at each step their difference from materials received in other ways. If selectors review the books individually, shipments must be prepared (and likely pre-screened for duplication and errors) and set out in an accessible area, in some kind of subject grouping, generally by call number as provided by the vendor on slips accompanying the books, for selectors to review on a regular basis. A shipment may remain on review for one week before being replaced by the next. This can place a considerable burden on the acquisitions staff, especially the person(s) responsible for maintaining the weekly review schedule. Nonetheless, the schedule must be adhered to because more books will be arriving from the vendor, in an unceasing flow.

The above discussion indicates that, while staff time is freed from certain tasks, other demands make "saving staff time" not as pure a benefit as is sometimes believed.

Tape loading of bibliographic records for approval books is clearly a great saver of staff time that would otherwise be spent in inputting a record for each approval book. In the University at Albany Libraries, online records are created manually for several small plans, while records for books received on three other plans are tape loaded. It takes a clerk an average of four minutes to search the database and create an approval record. During the period of July 1989 through June 1990, 7,896 records for books received on the two largest plans were tape loaded. These records would have taken 526.4 hours of clerical time if created manually. The actual loading of tapes requires about two minutes per tape of another department's time, totalling about three and one half hours if 52 tapes are provided in a year by each vendor. A student is on duty in case of problems while the tape is running, and it may take an hour to load a tape.

Coordinating a multiplicity of approval plans can be a daunting task. In fact, libraries have been known to abandon approval plans altogether when faced with overlap and duplication problems. Nevertheless, some hard work and care on the part of both libraries and vendors can reduce these sorts of problems. Knowledge of publishing and distribution will help to place publishers on the most appropriate plan. For example, Oxford University Press may be thought of as a British publisher, but it is in reality a global publisher that distributes all of its imprints in the United States.

Therefore, its publications can be included on a North American approval plan, where they will likely be supplied at a lower cost than if purchased abroad.

DISCOUNT

Although the common belief is that approval books are supplied at a higher discount than firm-ordered books, this may not always be the case. The materials included on the approval plan, the plan discount and the vendor that would be used if those same items were firm-ordered all work together to determine whether an approval plan provides an advantageous discount.

The University at Albany Libraries attempted to test this hypothesis by comparing the prices of 51 books actually received on approval to the prices that would have been charged for them by the library's major firm-order vendor. The approval plan supplied all but "net" titles at a 10 percent discount. The 51 test books would have been supplied at a discount of 12 percent. However, the firm-order vendor has offered an across-the-board flat rate of 15 percent.

VIEW FROM THE VENDOR'S SIDE

Vendors who offer approval plans consider them a desirable part of the business because they promise regular, dependable sales. Large standing orders can be placed with publishers and shipments can be expected automatically. Approval plans often beget other business, such as standing orders or firm-orders. But while they can be good for business, they are also expensive to maintain. The vendor must maintain records of each library's profile, shipping schedules, and other orders it may have. It must deal with shipments of returned books. And it must keep watch on publishers who may fail to make shipments or who may exclude some titles from shipment. It must meet with customers to discuss profiling changes, complaints, and other problems.

PROFILES

The profile—that document in which the library specifies what the vendor should supply in terms of subject area, publisher, country of origin, format, etc.—can be complex. Each vendor has its own method of profiling for a subject-based plan. It may be based on the Library of Congress classification scheme or a subject hierarchy developed by the vendor. It may be an elaborate computer-produced document or documents, it may be check marks next to LC numbers, or it may be a few sentences in a letter to the vendor. If the profile is fine tuned by subject area, the selector for each area must understand the ramifications of each decision. It also means that the profile will vary by subject area.

Monitoring the receipts may be done by other staff who need to understand the entire profile. As market conditions, publishers, libraries' priorities, and funding all change, the profiles change too. All staff involved need to keep abreast of such changes. Selectors, in particular, need to be aware of changes that would necessitate alterations in profile. If a college or university begins a new program, a collection will need to be built for it and the approval plan profile(s) adjusted to include appropriate materials. Ideally, adjustments to profiles are done in anticipation of needs, since it takes time to effect changes in a profile and to see those changes reflected in book shipments. The vendor's task of matching books to library profile—applying descriptors to a book and/or deciding whether a book fits a profile—is an intricate and imperfect art.

MANAGEMENT REPORTS

Vendors offering approval plans also provide management reports, which can be very useful collection management tools. These reports, which are generally quarterly, summarize shipments, library purchases, and returns by subject area showing both numbers of books and prices. Such data are an indication of average prices of books; overall expenditures for the plan; expenditures by subject area; and numbers of books provided, accepted, and returned overall and by subject.

IS AN APPROVAL PLAN DESIRABLE?

Approval plans are a widespread and accepted means of acquiring monographs in academic libraries. As has been pointed out, they can assure the library of obtaining a core of essential material; they eliminate the need for preparation of firm-orders for those titles; they can free selectors to pursue more obscure materials; and they can, to some extent, be budgeted for. Faculty members may be pleased to find desired books in the library without having been requested. On the other hand, approval plans do require maintenance. Acquisitions department staff must ensure that the vendor(s) adheres to the profile(s), while selectors must be alert to needed refinements in profile necessitated by changes in institutional policy and/or changes in the publishing industry.

After weighing these factors, one can decide whether a plan is desirable. If selectors do not wish to cooperate or staff to maintain the plan is unavailable, it will not work.

CHOOSING A PLAN

Two essentials precede the establishment of any approval plan: 1) clear understanding of the library's collecting goals and objectives, staffing levels, subject expertise, and political climate; and 2) thorough study of the literature on approval plans, which is quite extensive. Reidelbach and Shirk provide a thorough explication of the process of approval plan vendor selection and evaluation, which should be the starting point of one's review of the literature. Only after doing considerable homework should one begin to interview vendors.

Approval plans may be publisher-based or subject-based. In either case, the profile is the document that spells out what is and is not to be supplied. In a publisher-based plan all, or virtually all, of a publisher's output is supplied. Some restrictions can be established, and returns are allowed. The simplest and one of the most common publisher-based plans is the university press plan, in which all books published by university presses from a given list are supplied. The assumption is that such material is of a scholarly nature and therefore suitable for an academic library's collection, although reduced funding may necessitate a closer examination of such assumptions. Publisher-based plans use simple profiles and are easier for the vendor to maintain than are subject-based plans.

A publisher-based plan going beyond university presses has been used successfully at the University of Illinois at Urbana-Champaign library. Karen A. Schmidt found that such a plan makes better use of the expertise of selectors because they are freed to focus their attention on "identifying fugitive and difficult materials." Likewise, being intrinsically simpler than a subject-based plan, a publisher-based plan also demands less of the staff who oversee the mechanical aspects of the functioning of the plan. A simpler plan may also provide a higher discount.

Schmidt also found that, because of differences in the business of publishing outside North America, physical distance, and lack of knowledge on the part of North American librarians, foreign plans functioned better when subject-based. A subject-based plan, however, can be very complex, especially for a large library. Not only are specific subjects delineated, often by minute subdivisions, but they must be matched to a publisher list as well. Add to that various parameters of price, format, intended audience, conflict with the customer's standing orders, etc., and the result is an elaborate filter system through which a given book must pass before it is selected. Some subjects may be denoted as forms, while others are to be supplied as books. This will determine whether a book that passes successfully through the profiling parameters is sent to the library or only a notification form is sent.

A process of this complexity is prone to error. The simpler the profile, the easier it is to maintain the plan for all involved. It might be worthwhile to reduce the number of monographic series obtained on standing order and let the books arrive on approval instead, especially if they tend to be duplicated. Even if they are not being duplicated, receiving such material on approval permits review of each volume before it is added to the collection, as is seldom the case with standing orders.

A SPECIAL PARTNERSHIP

The manner in which a library manages its approval plan(s) directly relates to the relationship it establishes with the vendor.

Partners can become adversaries if the library demands more than can reasonably be expected from an approval plan. Likewise, the library can become a victim, even without any ill intent on the part of the vendor, if it does not carefully manage the plan.

Simply establishing a profile and letting the resulting books flow into the collection is no longer an option for many libraries. Accountability requires closer scrutiny of materials accepted for the collection.

Dissatisfaction and friction with the vendor will be unavoidable if the library has unrealistic expectations. The first year of a new approval plan will be difficult and will certainly result in more errors, profile refinements, and duplication and will require more time from both library and vendor than will subsequent years. One should build these eventualities into planning for the first year.

In terms of selection, an approval plan should be seen as a first line of collecting. Such a plan can build much of a core collection, but should not be expected to do more. It is a means of obtaining, readily, easily, and efficiently, books that the library would otherwise purchase by firm-order. That is, the plan provides books the library knows it wants. If a profile is purposely made very broad with the intent that it will bring into the library a vast range of books from which the library will then make its selections, the library is forcing the plan (and the vendor) to do something it cannot reasonably do. Used in this way, the plan becomes a selection tool, a substitute for working one's way through myriad reviews, flyers, and patron recommendations. The library is, in effect, saying: "Show us everything and we will see what we want." Very high return rates are the result, and, if consistently over 10 percent, they will be unacceptable to any vendor. There are costs to the library as well. The profile should be refined to the point where it provides what the library truly needs.

The library should not engage in a multitude of complaints: ask why an item was sent as a book rather as a form or vice versa, or why it was sent at all. The energy and expertise of selectors is better spent in searching out what the plan does not provide in order to maintain the breadth and depth of the collection consistent with collection development policy. Only major, consistent problems, such as in profile interpretation or duplication, should be a worry.

A recent study showed that approval plans provide far from perfect coverage, at least in science and technology. Of four vendors tested, the best supplied only 60.3 percent of the possible titles. Moreover, each of the four vendors supplied a significantly different assortment of books. Thus, there remains a great deal of selection to be done in conjunction with an approval plan. This study also underlines the significance of choice of vendor.

The vendor may, as a matter of policy, err on the side of generosity in supplying books that questionably fit the library's profile. This gives the library more to choose from and the vendor the possibility of more sales. If the library objects strenuously to this policy it should be discussed with the vendor, but the simpler course is to return unwanted material. Of course, consistently high return rates indicate that the plan is not supplying correct material and needs revision.

Overdependence on approval plans will limit a collection, just as overdependence on any single source will. Selectors must be synthesizers, collecting data from as broad a base as possible, sifting it, measuring it against collection development policy and systematically creating a collection suited to its clientele. Without assiduous augmentation of the collection beyond those materials supplied on approval plans, the selections made by the vendor's staff will shape the library's collections.

Much documentation on coverage provided by approval plans by subject areas is needed. Degrees of coverage will vary by subject, and consequently the nature of the selectors' activity will vary. Once they determine how a plan treats certain subjects, vendors and librarians can deal with questions relating to materials not covered by the plan. Suppose six vendors are surveyed for a particular subject and coverage varies by as much as 20 or 30 percent. One would ask why so much is missed and why the percentage varies. Is one vendor more successful than another, or are they in fact supplying what their respective customers desire? Are they all missing the same items or different ones? Should they supply what they are now missing? Would they be willing and/or able to do so? Would fuller coverage of the subject cost more than it would for selectors to fill in gaps with firm-ordered books? Such questions indicate how much there is to explore and how deeply entwined are the members of this partnership.

AUTOMATION

Vendors will provide what is demanded by their customers, and it seems that libraries increasingly want automated products. Given the ease with which bibliographic records can be provided through electronic transfer and tape loading, and the possibility of using CD-ROM technology for this as well, it only stands to reason that approval plans will benefit from advances in automation. Firm-ordered monographic titles, which may or may not be in a vendor's database and which will be supplied in numerous shipments over a period of time, do not lend themselves as well to this use of technology. However, it is much more feasible for a vendor to provide bibliographic records on tape for regular large shipments of books, all of which must be in the vendor's database since the vendor selected them. Thus, the benefits of automation and approval plan will augment each other and continue to shift some of the burden of record creation from library to vendor.

A FUTURISTIC VIEW

Martin Warzala, User Project Coordinator with Baker & Taylor Books Approval Program/Continuations Service System Development Project, provides the following picture of the approval plan in a personal communication. It is unfettered by today's technological limitations (which are rapidly being overcome) or by today's fixations on LC class number and publisher parameters. He points out that:

> ... use of approval plans in libraries has become more intricate, and vendors are developing more sophisticated features associated with the service.
>
> In general, the following services ... have become the rule, rather than the exception for providers of approval service: online access and/or searching and verification access to vendor approval files for titles in-process and/or treated on a vendor's approval plan (including client/profile-specific match information); machine-readable output including invoices, in-process acquisition records, and/or full MARC/ CIP records with approval service control elements; customer-defined elements, and/or invoice data in client specified fields and formats; ... electronically transmitted output, including invoices, in-process acquisition records, and/or full MARC/ CIP records with approval service control elements, customer-defined elements, and/or invoice data in client-specified fields and formats; ... and distribution of order/account processing function to the client's system, including profile-specific claiming and receipt of claim confirmation responses without

human intervention by vendor personnel, by direct contact with vendor systems.

. . . there has been, and will be, significant change based on client and market demands. Anticipated changes will be supported by further technological advances. In the short term, before 1995, library material vendors will continue to enhance/develop sophisticated levels of automation, database management, and bibliographic control, not only to support library material distribution, but to support information dissemination in a manner similar to but at a higher level than existing bibliographic utilities. . . . The more attractive sources of approval service will offer material coverage which is comprehensive and multinational in character. Material disseminated will not be restricted to traditional formats, but will include other recorded media. . . . They will become popular with appropriate control mechanisms and client-oriented packaging. Technical developments will support not only the above-noted library technical services functionality, but some distribution of profile creation and maintenance functions. These tasks will be performed by approval clients on their systems, without intervention by a vendor's personnel. There will be seamless interfaces with firm-order functions. . . . All functions distributed to libraries will be communicated from library systems to vendor systems via standard data transmission protocols. Thus a library's staff will be able to perform any approval-associated activity [on] . . . their own integrated library system. The combination of enhanced features will essentially make some vendors a "one stop source" for all library materials and associated bibliographic control services.

In the long term, post-2000, approval service will . . . more than likely resemble SDI (Selective Dissemination of Information) services, and material distribution will be an ancillary feature. The key capital expenditure in this environment, both for providers and users of the services, will be for information and communication, not material costs. Providers in the future will be analogous to gateways such as those used to access non-bibliographic databases. In addition to supporting fulfillment, search, and selection strategies, the future providers will distribute not only recorded media, but: parts of books; articles; and, data sets as required by the client user. . . . it will be dynamic and interactive. One speculates that the functionality will be distributed by institutions even closer to the end users

SUMMARY

To maximize good relations with an approval-plan vendor:

1. Prepare carefully and choose wisely.
2. Keep profile as simple as possible.
3. Avoid excessive pickiness.
4. Evaluate profile and performance continually.
5. Assiduously augment materials supplied on approval.

(or, perhaps directly to end users), and systems will utilize extremely objective determinants of collection management. In the academic environment, for example, future information systems may take into account information such as the number of faculty in a discipline, the number of students in a discipline at what grade level, circulation patterns, available budget funds, etc., to determine what material/information is ordered/requested from a provider's database/systems. Similar paradigms can be drawn for non-academic institutions. As we become even more advanced technologically, and as technological applications become more economical, the client may not even be an institution. Providers may deal directly with the end user, thus shortening the information dissemination chain significantly.

Solidly based on technological developments and the acceptance of standards as well as an expanding vision of the approval plan, this view of the future is exciting, challenging and, quite possibly, not too far-fetched. Should approval plans be provided as described above, there is no doubt that the librarian/vendor relationship will change.

8 OUT OF THE MAIN STREAM
NONPRINT MEDIA

Nonprint media in libraries used to mean audiovisual materials and microforms. Filmstrips, phonograph records, and microforms are difficult enough to acquire, catalog, use, lend, and house, but libraries must now choose from an array of other media vying for their places in library budgets and collections. Audiocassettes, compact disks, CD-ROMs, video disks, magnetic tapes, and software programs have moved into libraries of all types, placing heavy demands on limited budgets. These new media continue to grow in popularity. CD-ROM in particular is increasingly seen as a medium with a bright future in information delivery and processing. Libraries are now on the threshold of yet another form of publishing as well: electronic publishing. As with earlier nonprint media, these new media are seen as adjuncts to book and periodical collections. Even electronic publishing is not expected to eliminate the printed word, although CD-ROMs and electronic formats are sometimes touted as the means of saving libraries both funds and space. Much information can certainly be neatly contained on CD-ROM disks, occupying a fraction of the space of printed materials. Electronic publishing is sometimes seen as the death knell of the printed word, but it is not difficult to recall that microforms were once, mistakenly, expected to do the same.

The newest media have already been embraced by the public, often well ahead of libraries. Most library patrons have used audiocassettes and videocassettes elsewhere. Children use computers from grade school onward. The use of home computers is widespread. And scholars are rapidly adopting electronic mail as a means of communication. Some college and university campuses provide each student and faculty member with a personal computer and linkage to the scholarly community at large. CD-ROM databases cannot be provided fast enough to satisfy demand. Publishers recognize that the market is user-driven, and they will provide what end users want. Libraries have established multimedia centers where these new formats can be used in either a passive or interactive mode, one medium at a time or several integrated. Libraries themselves are finding videos and software a useful means of communicating with their clientele. Video library tours are popular and hypercard/hypertext-based self-teaching programs are also proving useful and popular. Libraries will find themselves increasingly caught between their users' demands for new media and constraints on their ability to respond. It remains to be seen whether electronic publishing will fulfill its promise or whether, on a large scale, it will lose its novelty and run into resistance from users who become disenchanted with extensive reading from a monitor. More and more interactive applications appear to lie ahead, with knowledge, not just information being the ultimate goal.

Investment in equipment for these new media can be tremendous and may be linked to the purchase of specific materials, making such costs impossible to postpone. Common processing tasks such as barcoding, labelling, security stripping, and shelving can present challenges that can absorb inordinate amounts of time. Questions of archival copies and copyright arise. All of this means that patrons will demand more of libraries and that libraries and their vendors may have a very difficult time keeping up with rapidly changing needs.

SUPPLIERS OF TRADITIONAL NONPRINT MATERIALS

Many libraries, especially school and public libraries, have well-established sources of supply for phonograph records, films, and microforms. They probably have acceptable sources of equipment as well. Nevertheless, this is a problematic area and a reliable supplier is to be valued highly. Published since 1969, *The AV Market Place* (Bowker) has continually evolved with the market and has provided not only a comprehensive guide to available materials and their publishers, but has also served as a barometer of the development of the AV field. A number of book vendors supply AV materials; those that do can be identified in the *Literary Market Place* (Bowker) or by querying one's preferred vendor directly.

Microforms have assumed an enduring role within libraries, although user resistance and equipment problems remain. Newspapers and periodicals, research collections, and material in need of preservation are commonly retained in microform. The *Microform Market Place* (Veaner and Meckler) currently lists over 400 publishers. Microforms are generally purchased directly from publishers rather than through vendors.

SUPPLIERS OF NEWER NONPRINT MATERIALS

Many libraries have found it difficult to shift priorities and funds to incorporate new media. Whereas aging phonograph record collections could be replaced incrementally at relatively low cost, the advent of music on compact disks meant starting over again and replacing equipment as well. Libraries committed to maintaining music collections have little choice since many performances are now issued on compact disks rather than records.

When one's vendor lacks established contact with a video publisher and material is needed quickly, the library is likely to order direct from the publisher. Even vendors who do supply nonbook formats may not supply a broad range because of the rapidity with which publishers and products proliferate, lack of standardization, uncertain markets, and other problems.

Even when ordering from a vendor known to supply nonbook formats there are often problems. If the vendor maintains a database of compact disks, for example, it will be immensely useful for the library to have a catalog or printout of available titles prior to ordering. In this way, the vendor's order number can be supplied. This is in fact the only definite identifier of a title, other than the publisher's own number, which may be unavailable, not unique, or not accessed in the database. Unless selection is made from the vendor's list, it may still be difficult to match desired items with the list. Libraries have received duplicate CDs and videos simply because of the use of differing titles in different reviewing and advertising sources. In addition, the proliferation of publishers in this field makes it difficult for vendors to establish and maintain contact with them.

When purchasing such materials, librarians can use one of their usual book suppliers or order direct from the publisher or specialized distributor. If a book vendor can supply such material, that route will be by far the simplest. If, on the other hand, the library's preferred supplier does not handle such media or cannot obtain certain items, the library must deal directly with media publishers and distributors. This increases the library's workload, generally more so than does direct ordering of books. Numerous publishers of media must be dealt with, must be informed of library policies and requirements, and must be paid. If preview copies of videos are needed, they must usually be returned since different copies are sold. There may be a fee for previewing as well as the cost of shipping. When the purchased copy is received, payment will be made in the usual manner. If this is slow, these publishers may not be very understanding.

The University at Albany Libraries spent $10,000 on videos about cultural diversity with several months still remaining in the fiscal year. It was necessary to order 38 titles from 25 different publishers and one library book supplier. Another 17 titles were previewed and returned but not purchased. When the fiscal year ended, 13 titles had not yet been received. Small amounts of money had to be encumbered for each of 12 publishers. Had these been ordered from a library vendor, they might have been supplied more quickly, and encumbering would definitely have been simpler—just one lump sum for the vendor, which might also have included funds for books not yet received. A remarkable amount of staff time was absorbed in placing and monitoring these few orders. Each publisher was a new entity to be added to the online acquisitions system. Some required prepayment, which entails delays in obtaining an invoice, having a check cut and returned to the library for mailing with the order, and subsequent tracking of the item. Some publishers failed to comply with library terms stated on the order form such as returning one copy of the order form with the item or supplying a three-part invoice. This is an instance where the services of a library vendor were sorely missed. Had consolidation of these orders been possible with one of the library's regular suppliers, much time and effort could have been saved.

More recently traditional book suppliers have begun to embrace other media, and some specialized dealers have emerged who offer, for example, cassettes and compact disks with attractive pricing and incentives designed to appeal to libraries.

CD-ROM

When CD-ROM (Compact Disk Read-Only Memory) burst on the library scene in the mid-1980s, most libraries were ill prepared. Some tried to ignore it, hoping it would go away. It does not seem likely to do so, except in the sense that it will move into more sophisticated applications. Whatever form it takes, it cannot be ignored.

CD-ROMs may contain texts that were difficult to use in print format, such as an encyclopedia or the Bible. Others contain data files such as census data. Those that have had the greatest impact on library services have been the CD-ROM indexes. In all cases, searching for needed information has been transformed. Laboriously going through many issues of an index, for instance, reading fine print in search of an elusive citation is slow, tedious, and imperfect. Online searching, while effective, generally requires the assistance of a trained searcher, and costs may be charged to the patron. CD-ROM, however, is more user friendly than either of these. CD-ROM publishers see great potential beyond current products, with more powerful personal computers (PCs) and CD-ROMs providing an unsophisticated user with seamless access to a varied and integrated fund of information. At the present time, the audio capacity of CD-ROM can permit a user to listen to a piece of music while reading the score on a computer screen. CD-ROM can also be linked to videos, providing the opportunity to view works of art or architectural images and accompanying text.

CD-ROM publishers understand that they can create demand by adding value and ultimately increase profits through increasing sales and by adding adjunct products. They have also seen that CD-ROM products have not supplanted print versions of the databases, but have been added sales. A good example of such a value-added product is *Books In Print Plus*, which appears to be *Books In Print* in a different format. However, one use is sufficient to convince anyone that it can do far more, faster and more easily than the print version. Does a patron want to know what books are available on the Celts or Celtic heritage? A simple search provides the answer in seconds and the push of a button prints it out. Users have choices—brief or full citations, full publisher information, etc. Who would choose to extract this information laboriously from the fine print in the *Subject Guide to Books In Print*, given this option? Libraries will find it difficult indeed to keep such powerful tools from an increasingly demanding and aware public.

From the acquisitions viewpoint, the impact has included funding questions, difficulties in dealing directly with a variety of CD-ROM publishers and sometimes, in addition, the originators of the database, problems of check-in, handling, and returning of disks that fit no existing routines for books or serials. Many other issues revolve around CD-ROM, including questions of ownership of the data, licensing agreements, standards, usage, preservation, and training and support.

ELECTRONIC PUBLISHING

Electronic publishing is moving into the serials world and cannot be ignored by serials vendors, nor is the electronic monograph far in the future. More than 50 dictionaries are available in electronic format. No fewer than 60 electronic publishers are identified in the 1990 *Ulrich's Plus* database. Electronic publishing encompasses original prose materials disseminated solely online (possibly with optional print copy available on request), non-bibliographic data files such as statistical files, and services such as the Dow-Jones News/Retrieval Service. Some of the leading publishers in this area are not traditional servers of the library market. Dow Jones and H & R Block's CompuServe Information Service are marketed directly to homes and businesses. Others, such as Dialog, Lexis, Nexis, and Medis are somewhat more comfortable with the library community, but they are nevertheless outside the mainstream of library materials purchases. Can such electronic products be absorbed into that mainstream through the concerted efforts of librarians and their traditional suppliers?

This question will likely not be resolved in this century, but discussion of electronic publishing cannot fail to make the issue of commercial versus non-commercial production of journals increasingly significant to the scholarly community. Scholarly journals are being produced now in a variety of ways without any standards in place. Some may be purchased through a commercial network like CompuServe. Some may maintain an office staff, sell subscriptions, and be issued in more than one format. Others may remain entirely free, produced by the scholars themselves, distributed on BITNET or Internet, which link institutions and which mandate free access. It is expected that sometime in the future, all educational institutions will be linked electronically through The National Research and Education Network (NREN) or something akin to it. In order to be useful to the wider community, they must be indexed and accessible.

It is clearly inevitable that electronic publishing will have a major impact on the relationship between librarians and their suppliers, even though in a fundamental sense the agents' role may remain as it is now: facilitator of the supply of information.

GOVERNMENT PUBLICATIONS

Documents emanating from various local, state, federal, and foreign government agencies and international bodies such as the United Nations present many challenges to the acquisitions department. Generally, a separate unit is established to handle these materials. Because they are not purchased, United States federal documents issued by the Superintendent of Documents are seldom handled through normal acquisitions channels. Some book and serials suppliers provide government publications to libraries. Some book vendors have GPO, NTIS, United Nations, Canadian, and certain overseas documents. In fact, some dealers focus entirely on government publications. Such dealers may be best located through recommendations of librarians who have used them successfully as they may not appear in standard book trade sources. Many documents are best or solely obtained from their sources.

In recent years, there has been a movement away from print documents. Microforms were used by the United States federal government as a cost-saving measure, resulting in delayed availability of information and production of poor quality fiche.

The National Technical Information Service database has been available online from Dialog since 1972. Now this database of citations and abstracts for reports on government research and development work is also available on CD-ROM. The occupational health and safety data from NIOSH, as well as British and United Nations sources, is available on OSH-ROM; the AGRICOLA database from the National Agricultural Library is also available on CD-ROM. NASA, the United States Geological Survey, the Federal Deposit Insurance Corporation, the National Institutes of Health, and the Internal Revenue Service all offer CD-ROM products. Considerable census information from the United States and other countries is also available on CD-ROM. Fortunately, the relationship between depository libraries and the Government Printing Office is generally good. Libraries have input when changes are considered and are forewarned about new formats and other developments. Federal documents can be in any format—print, CD-ROM, online, floppy disk—and increasingly they are in nonprint formats. Despite problems to the library attendant on such formats, the information in documents is much more accessible to the user in electronic format than on paper. Money seems more available to fund electronic projects, and generally libraries favor them. That the United States federal government is moving into CD-ROM and other formats with some enthusiasm should be apparent from the fact that the Government Printing Office has an Information Technology Program headed by a librarian responsible for researching, developing, and implementing a plan for the application of modern information technologies in the Federal Depository Library Program.

Because of the United States government policy of contracting out publishing, government databases, which might once have resulted in the issuance of federal documents, become transformed into CD-ROM serials available from the commercial sector. They are not true documents any longer, although they contain government data. This complicates the documents picture because many documents, especially those other than United States federal documents, continue to appear in print.

THE PARTNERSHIP

Given the bibliographic and supply problems faced by libraries and vendors in managing the acquisition of such things as audiocassettes, videoscassettes, CDs, and CD-ROMs, is there a course of action they could pursue together that would improve the situation? It seems that book suppliers must include other media. Libraries need consolidated sources for the variety of materials they must purchase, and some book vendors have moved into this area, but addition of new media to one's inventory is not a simple matter. Contact with publishers must be made and relationships established; databases must absorb nonbook descriptions; questions of warehousing must be considered. There is no title page, no ISBN. It is clear that bibliographic standardization would ease distribution. If vendors and librarians could jointly engage publishers in discussions of the value of this, perhaps progress could be made.

Substantial publishers of nonprint media may carve their own niches and develop good working knowledge of and relationships with the library community, much as University Microfilms has done in the microform and document delivery field. However, proliferation of small publishers with differing policies and little awareness of library needs will not serve the library community well. Such fragmentation of the market will continue to increase library problems and work loads by preventing vendors from providing the very services of consolidation and ease of communication for which libraries value them.

The same is true of subscription agents, who should be equipped to supply any titles available on a subscription or standing order basis, regardless of format. CD-ROM in particular is an example of a new medium that appeared suddenly and rapidly assumed a major role in information delivery. Electronic publishing will likely be next. Libraries wanting consolidated serials service welcome the provision of CD-ROM subscriptions through agents, but there are questions of service charges (which can be substantial given the high cost of these items) and actual servicing of the subscription to be considered. As in the case of print subscriptions, the agent is a facilitator, but given the more complex nature of CD-ROM subscriptions there is more to facilitate and it may be more difficult to do it well. There may be hardware involved, the publisher may provide installation and training; and disks may need to be returned directly to the publisher, as will license agreements. Thus, the library must deal with both the subscription agent and the publisher.

This situation raises questions regarding the viability of vendors: Will they be able to supply the full range of materials needed by libraries? Will they adjust to changing markets in the future? The past decade has already seen the demise of a number of vendors. However, the library market is diverse and has long required a diversity of vendors to supply it. If there are libraries that can be best served by no-frills book suppliers, for instance, it will be up to these libraries to form viable partnerships with such vendors. In

SUMMARY

To make the most of nonprint suppliers:

1. Encourage traditional materials suppliers to provide nonprint materials.
2. Work with newer sources to broaden their understanding of library markets.

doing business with those vendors who best suit their particular situations, libraries can encourage the existence of a healthy diversity among vendors.

Contracts and license agreements for nontraditional media such as videos and CD-ROMs and other machine-readable data files present problems as well. Even when these materials are supplied by a vendor, the vendor plays no role in the licensing agreements. It has been interesting to note that those few publishers with knowledge of the library community have produced the simplest and least restrictive license agreements, while other publishers are likely to come up with very complex agreements. Acquisitions librarians are in a poor position when faced with such agreements. They cannot enforce the terms, and they may lack the authority to sign. Before attempting to deal with such a contract or agreement, the librarian should ascertain who in the institution is legally able to sign an agreement on behalf of the library. It may be one indemnified person in the institution. If the librarian signs, he or she may be signing for himself or herself, not on behalf of the institution. Some institutions alter agreements before signing them, which some publishers may find objectionable. The library may find itself unable to purchase an item if the two parties cannot agree on terms.

Perhaps vendors and librarians could join forces here to make a case for the simplest type of agreement. If a few publishers are able to accept a simple agreement, do others really need several pages of fine print? University Microfilms, perhaps due to its extensive experience in supplying library markets, provides clear, simple license agreements in print that is large enough to be seen without a magnifying glass.

Libraries will be best served if they can purchase as many different types of media as possible successfully through library suppliers with whom they have established working relationships. It will not be easy. As has been pointed out, proliferation of media and their publishers, can make it difficult for vendors to fill their old roles in the new modes. These new media are being marketed directly to their users. Librarians and their vendors are being challenged and will have to work together to determine what the best methods of supply should be in order to satisfy the information needs of library patrons.

9 OUT-OF-PRINT

In the past, librarians have often viewed antiquarian booksellers somewhat negatively—making money from those precious tomes that belong in rare book collections. In fact, librarians have often deliberately kept deaccessioned materials from these book dealers, so as not to support this once thought dubious business.

In recent years, however, "out-of-print" has become a familiar phrase among librarians, who have seen that books go out of print faster than they once did and that press runs are shorter, particularly for scholarly materials. Thus, librarians have begun to look toward the out-of-print market to find books they did not acquire when they were in print, or books that have been irreparably damaged or lost. Dealers in such books use various terms to describe themselves—antiquarian, old, used, rare, second-hand. The used book may not be out-of-print, while the out-of-print, if remaindered, may be new. Be that as it may, librarians seldom organize their selection or purchasing practices with such dealers in mind. In fact, they seldom give the out-of-print market much thought at all, unless they are rare book librarians or are purchasing for highly specialized collections. Being disorganized and sporadic in one's approach to out-of-print buying does a disservice both to the library community and to the out-of-print bookseller.

It is obviously much simpler and cheaper to buy a book while it is in print—which is one reason for maintaining adequate funds for books in acquisitions budgets. Administrators need to understand the logic of this, and librarians need to understand the intricacies of out-of-print buying in order to do it when necessary—and to make the case for its avoidance. The need for out-of-print materials will probably increase as collections age, budgets remains tight, student populations increase, and print runs remain short. Librarians must recognize that the out-of-print dealer can become as worthwhile a partner as the traditional library supplier of in-print materials.

If librarians are sometimes guilty of making unreasonable demands of suppliers of in-print materials, they are often perceived as making outrageous demands of out-of-print dealers. Some dealers are former librarians; most are genuinely fond of books and whatever related materials they choose to sell such as old periodicals, trade catalogs, photographs, and other ephemera. Most are as serious about their work as librarians are about theirs, and as upright and dependable. But here the two professions diverge in their language, organization, outlook, and expectations.

LIBRARIANS VS. BOOK DEALERS

Librarians are notorious for their focus on detail to the end of organizing the vast body of knowledge in a way that will make it accessible to those who seek it. They employ uniform codes of bibliographic description, and no online public catalog is considered complete without authority control. At the same time, they are often perceived as being routine-oriented and inflexible. Moreover, they are more often than not embedded in rigid and demanding bureaucracies over whose business practices they have little control.

Contrast this to the out-of-print book dealer, who in most cases has no training or experience that would give him or her a similar base. The booksellers come from a variety of educational backgrounds and may simply translate love of books into a way of life. Some catalogs are neat, legible, informative, and organized in a useful manner; some are not. Moreover, the dealer in out-of-print books exists in numerous and fragmented form all over North America. The fragmentation of this market, its constantly changing makeup, and the inevitable variety from one dealer to another is dictated by its very nature. There is no source, no publisher, no distribution system for the out-of-print. This is an unusual situation indeed, one that is bound to try the best-laid plans of the acquisitions librarian who does not focus specifically on this market, adapt to it, and utilize it sensibly and fairly.

A WHOLE NEW WORLD

It is incumbent upon librarians to educate themselves about the out-of-print market. After all, they want to buy these books, but they are likely be demanding customers—at least compared to the dealer's usual customers who are delighted to find a longed-for book, pay for it with a check or credit card, and be happy with a simple receipt. This process of self-education is not difficult and can be downright enjoyable. Librarians can begin by looking at such publications as the *AB Bookman's Weekly*, the *AB Bookman's Yearbook*, and *Literary Market Place*. Specific dealers can be identified through these publications as well as through *Buy Books Where—Sell Books Where: A Directory of Out of Print Book-*

sellers and Their Author-Subject Specialties. But identifying dealers is not the only goal. A little investigation will quickly reveal a dimension to the book business other than the in-print market. Listings in the *AB Bookman's Weekly* give dates and locations for antiquarian book fairs all over the country. Other shows may be advertised locally. What better way to learn about these dealers than to meet and talk with them, handle their wares, get to know them on their own turf? Love of what they do keeps them going to these events. What else can explain their repeated packing, unpacking, loading, and carting of heavy books and assorted display paraphernalia? Nevertheless, librarians with "want lists" in hand, and prepared to buy, are rare at antiquarian book fairs.

Librarians can also benefit from attending the Out-Of-Print & Antiquarian Book Market Seminar held in Denver each year. This is without a doubt the most intensive and mind-expanding introduction to the antiquarian book trade available and results in tremendously stimulating exchanges between book sellers and librarians.

OUT-OF-PRINT STATUS

Books found in *Books in Print* but reported out-of-print by a library supplier or books with recent imprint dates not appearing in *BIP* can often be searched by the supplier who reported them out-of-print. Such a vendor can be requested to do an OP search automatically on any item that he or she is reporting out-of-print, or the library may choose to make an item-by-item decision as titles are reported out-of-print. If the first option fails to produce the book, the vendor will cancel the order and the library can then pursue it through out-of-print channels. These are often scholarly titles, not originally expensive, but often hard to find.

Rare books, on the other hand, may be anywhere from several years to hundreds of years old and may carry impressive price tags. These are the ones both dealers and librarians keep under lock and key. Fortunate indeed is the library that can maintain an active collecting program in its chosen areas of rare book purchasing, sending a knowledgeable librarian out on the road to auctions and estate sales, buying items by telephone from dealers' catalogs, and favored with the efforts of specialized dealers. Rare books are often works of art, often the foundation upon which modern scholarship rests. Nevertheless, for most of us, the recently out-of-print is a more realistic part of everyday work, equally challenging in its pursuit and equally valuable to the library user.

Perhaps the most unwelcome delay in the ordering process is the out-of-print report because of its apparent finality. Someone may be waiting to use the book; encumbered funds are left in limbo; and acquisitions staff may be hard-pressed to find time to pursue a nebulous quest. When a book is reported out-of-print, acquisitions staff should have clear parameters within which to work. The simplest and cheapest approach is to consider the order cancelled, but this also provides the poorest service to library users.

Vendors report that books are out-of-print because publishers tell them so, but there are any number of possible reasons for this. The clerk at the publishing house may have been in error; there may be other errors at the publisher's end; the warehouse may have lacked the title one day, only to have a large number of books returned from bookstores the next day. It is worthwhile asking the vendor to pursue the title further with the publisher, even to reorder the title from another vendor, and to call the publisher to verify the book's status. (Vendors who habitually report out-of-print just those titles they do not want to supply should not be used.) Having exhausted these possibilities, the library must either consider the order dead or find other channels to pursue.

REMAINDERS

Although remainders dealers may be able to supply needed books, they may be difficult for libraries to deal with, and it may be difficult to determine who has what. Both Baker & Taylor and Ingram purchase bulk remainder stock from publishers. Other remainders dealers, less familiar to most librarians, are listed in *Literary Market Place*.

Bibliographers may select from remainder catalogs and publishers' sale lists. If potential problems in doing business with these firms are resolved in advance, they can provide needed material on the verge of going out of print at low prices.

ORGANIZING OP PURCHASING

In a small library, the librarian may select and purchase all materials for the collection and will need to be familiar with library suppliers of in-print as well as out-of-print materials. Out-of-print buying may seldom occur, or it may be an important focus of the acquisitions program. In larger libraries, a unit may be set up solely for this purpose and may deal with a variety of rare and out-of-print book sellers on a regular basis. In some libraries, budgetary restraints make out-of-print purchasing all but nonexistent.

Unfortunately, the librarian's penchant for organization fails when it comes to organizing out-of-print purchasing. If a library has seriously considered the issue and concluded that it really cannot do better than to order out-of-print materials in the same way that it orders in-print items, it will have to accept the resulting low success rate for its out-of-print orders. An organized and flexible approach, however, can benefit almost every library that does any out-of-print buying.

The library must first know what out-of-print buying it will do. It is not necessary to perform out-of-print searches for all unavailable material when options such as microfilming and photo duplication exist. Likewise, in an era of rising serials costs, fax machines, full-text document delivery, and resource sharing, it is hardly wise to hunt for every missing periodical issue. Not only will the material, if found, be costly, but the process itself is expensive. Clear policies must exist, as well as criteria for applying them.

THE TOLL ON ACQUISITIONS STAFF

Out-of-print buying makes considerable demands on the acquisitions department. Staff members must be knowledgeable about potential sources, be prepared for extra difficulty, delay, and reordering, while at the same time expediting the ordering process within the library. It is an expensive process, in terms of staff time, and may yield nothing despite months, if not years, of effort. If a dealer is asked to search indefinitely, any number of items may be on order with little expectation that they will arrive in the current fiscal year or any other. This can present some difficulties if fiscal management is rigidly controlled at the library.

Because of the special knowledge required and the need for expeditious treatment of the ordering and payment, obtaining out-of-print materials should be the responsibility of one person or unit with the time and dedication to devote to it. If mixed with regular orders or dealt with as fallout from unfilled firm-orders, out-of-print purchasing is bound to be ineffective. No better explanation of the rationale for a well organized, knowledgeable approach exists than Joe Barker's article "Organizing Out-Of-Print and Replacement Acquisitions for Effectiveness, Efficiency, and the Future." Careful study of Barker's clearly reasoned and explained approach will benefit any library, large or small.

UNDERSTANDING THE BUSINESS

Before attempting to buy from an out-of-print dealer, it is essential that the library and the vendor understand each other's methods of doing business. Dealers may be willing to hold books pending receipt of a purchase order, but for how long? Assuring dealers that a purchase order will arrive within two weeks and then berating them for selling the book elsewhere after waiting for four or six weeks is unreasonable. Can they produce the number of invoice copies the institution requires? Will they ship and bill (and be patient), or is payment required with the order? Payment with order is not an unreasonable expectation for a small business.

TIME AND THE OP BOOK

Time and price parameters must be understood. Libraries must recognize that speed of delivery of such material is less important than ultimate success in the search. If an OP item is wanted for reserve reading, the professor may think the book should appear immediately. The librarian may query several dealers by phone to see if anyone has the book in stock. It may then arrive in the library in a week or two. However, a lengthy search is almost inevitable, especially for academic material.

For one thing, these books are elusive. The book on the iodamoeba that the professor has put on his reserve reading list went out of print four years ago after a brief life. Those who bought it were interested in the subject and are keeping the book. The recent OP book may be rarer than some "rare" books. The second reason is that out-of-print dealers are not as well organized as libraries. They may not know exactly what they have boxed in storage, or they may think they have a particular book but are unable to locate it.

It is important to give the dealer as much time as it takes to produce the book. Likewise, claiming—especially regular automatic claims produced by online acquisitions systems—have a negative effect. If the dealer had found the book, the library would have been contacted.

PRICE AND THE OP BOOK

Librarians must be willing to pay for the books they order. An OP search may involve the placement of ads, the production and mailing of lists, and any number of long-distance telephone calls. Dealers have other overhead, plus the price they must pay for the book, and a mark-up for profit. Either establish a maximum price at the outset (one based on the reality of the OP book business), or give the dealer *carte blanche* to charge a fair price for the book. If a book is not truly essential to the collection and the library is only willing to spend a pittance on it, there is no point in ordering it.

Giving the dealer free rein is not as dangerous as it might seem at first. A librarian who is knowledgeable about the out-of-print market will recognize a fair price, and a dealer knows that price gouging will mean no more orders from that library. A library that can set realistic price limits or allow the dealer leeway will receive faster results because the dealer will not have to quote before supplying the book. If quotes are necessary, the acquisitions librarian should respond rapidly.

Various creative ways can be developed for utilizing limited library funds while giving the dealer a fair amount of business. Deposit accounts are one way. If a fixed amount has been budgeted for a given period, tell the dealer the amount and then send quantities of orders, the goal being to get as many books from the group as possible for available funds. Once a trusting relationship exists between dealer and librarian, it is possible to explore such options and to come up with creative and mutually beneficial ideas.

CONDITION AND THE OP BOOK

Libraries are seldom satisfied with anything less than "as new" or very close to it. Doing an expensive, time-consuming search only to obtain a book whose pages are too fragile to permit use is foolish. Other alternatives such as microfilm should be considered first.

Condition should be dealt with when the order is placed. Only if a book is received in a condition markedly different from that described by the dealer is the library justified in rejecting it. Description of a book's condition is a subjective art. Terminology and definitions appearing in the *AB Bookman's Weekly* may not be universally agreed upon or adhered to, nor is there any mechanism for forcing uniformity of usage. When first setting up parameters of doing business, make sure that the dealer knows the library's policy on such things as hardcover versus paperback, marginal notes, and other marks in the book.

MATCHING NEEDS TO AVAILABLE TITLES

Traditionally, there have been two imperfect ways for connecting a library's needs with available OP books: the dealers' lists or catalogs sent to libraries, and the libraries' lists or orders sent to dealers. Most libraries use both methods. Neither is very effective when one considers the vast numbers of used books for sale by multitudinous dealers, but until recently that was all there was unless the librarian went book hunting in person.

Dealers' Catalogs: In order to purchase from catalogs, the library must be on the mailing lists of various dealers and must know what it wants. This means assembling a list, keeping it up to date, and leaving it in the hands of those who can act quickly and with authority when a catalog arrives. When a catalog arrives it must be checked immediately. Whether this is best done manually or by establishing a database must be determined by each library. A good discussion of a successful and relatively simple use of an in-house database is found in David Nuzzo's article "A Reasonable Approach to Out-Of-Print Procurement Using dBASE II or dBASE III." On the other hand, Joe Barker at Berkeley has found it more useful to keep lists in manual form.

Catalogs may also be used simply as selection tools by bibliographers who select out-of-print material just as they do anything else, rather than actually comparing a catalog to a "want list." In situations like this it can be virtually impossible to order quickly enough to obtain desired items. A special effort must be made to organize and streamline both the decision-making and ordering processes for such material. In some libraries, it may not only take time to produce a purchase order, it may be impossible to produce payment to accompany it.

Nevertheless, it is important to order quickly. Special procedures should be established and personnel assigned specifically to deal with OP material. It *is* possible to circumvent some red tape. Orders can be placed by telephone or fax, or typed with the appropriate signature. Procedures like updating files and online systems, and capturing fund accounting data, can be done afterward.

Library Lists: Libraries have an alternative to waiting for dealers' catalogs. They can and should place their orders with carefully selected dealers and give them leeway to proceed. Such orders should be as bibliographically complete as any other. The same list can be sent simultaneously to several dealers *if* the library is simply asking them to check their stock on hand and quote but do no actual searching. If an active search is required, the list should go to one carefully selected dealer who will be expected to pursue it over a long period of time. A dealer can be asked to advertise in journals such as the *AB Bookman's Weekly* or *The Library Bookseller*. Libraries can also place their own advertisements for desired materials.

WHICH DEALER AND HOW MANY?

A library needs to know which dealer or dealers are most likely to be able to supply needed OP items. Specialized titles should go to dealers in those subjects (art, botany, Russian-language material, etc.). Unless a library has the flexibility to function like an individual customer, without demanding numerous invoice copies and the like, it had best seek out dealers with some experience in selling to libraries. Academic libraries will want a general dealer in academic materials. Few dealers have much foreign-language material unless they specialize in it. A good "mix" works best for general dealers. A group of orders on various subjects in English is more likely to result in some books being supplied than one order on a subject in German. Science is particularly difficult because few OP dealers are scientists. If the library cannot produce a mix of orders, the dealer may never be able to supply a book. The library may judge the dealer harshly, but unreasonably. Some titles are unlikely ever to appear in an OP dealer's stock, such as collections originally targeted to the library market. Those sets will rest forever on library shelves, far from the OP dealer. The librarian has homework to do, references to check, questions to ask, parameters to establish.

Although a number of dealers may be used according to their specialities, it makes no sense to move orders from one dealer to another in the hope that one may succeed where another failed. A general dealer who is willing to deal with a particular library, who has a good reputation among librarians, with a sizable stock and several hundred "connections" for searches, is a good bet. Give that dealer your business and let him or her do what is possible. There are many interconnections. Dealers buy from each other; major in-print vendors who offer OP searching may use the same dealer the library uses on its own.

Selecting an OP dealer is quite different from selecting a vendor for in-print books. The latter is likely to be familiar with selling to libraries, while the out-of-print dealer may be a novice in this area. While many in-print vendors can supply the same books at similar prices, no OP dealer can guarantee to supply a particular book. Price and service offered by the OP dealer are less important than the subjects that dealer specializes in and the way the library itself functions.

BUILDING RELATIONSHIPS

In educating themselves about this side of the book supply business, librarians must overcome any negative prejudices they harbor and act as cooperative partners. This means sending orders to appropriate dealers, giving them adequate time to search, being realistic about prices, not inundating dealers with claims, not changing one's mind after a book has been located, paying promptly, and giving the dealer a fair amount of business.

Attempt to find dealers who target the library market. Other libraries buying OP material in similar subject areas can easily name their sources. A new horticulture librarian, for example, can gain recommendations, warnings, and insights with a few phone calls to librarians in other horticultural libraries. This knowledge can then be used as a basis for beginning to develop his or her own relationships with dealers.

A partnership established with an OP dealer is bound to be more personal than one forged with a large vendor of in-print materials. One may become very friendly with a customer service representative or a sales rep at an in-print house, but he or she will be only part of a large whole. An OP book dealer is often a one-person operation, who can work for the library if the librarian can motivate him or her to do so. Dealers can go beyond merely checking lists against their stock or selling books from their catalogs. They can actively search out books in subject areas known to be of interest, provide discounts, and perform appraisals of gifts the library receives. But dealers must know that there will be rewards—sales and future orders coupled with fair treatment along the way.

It is up to the librarian to make this relationship work. If you can establish a good rapport with a dealer or dealers, you will get better results. It is not necessary to have unlimited funds and multitudinous orders to be a good customer. More important are an understanding of the OP business, some common sense, and perhaps some creativity in circumventing institutional rigidity.

BACK ISSUES OF SERIALS

Obtaining back issues of serials poses special problems for the out-of-print buyer. The kind of serials most often sought by libraries—usually single issues of periodicals—are not often found in out-of-print dealers' catalogs. Although some do list issues of periodicals, these are destined for special collections, not the bound periodicals collection. Research libraries in particular look for serials that few others have any interest in. A special market has developed to supply just this material. Matching needs is not easy, and prices are likely to be high. Not infrequently, libraries must purchase an entire volume even though they need only a single issue. For this reason, it is important to have clearly defined policies regarding the bound periodicals collection. Maintaining a complete collection, fully bound, may not make sense in light of other options such as cooperative collection development, microforms, interlibrary loan, and full-text document delivery.

Prompt claiming will eliminate the need for some back-issue purchasing. A library may have greater success claiming directly with the publisher than through the subscription agent supplying the titles, a rather radical departure from common practice. Or, a library may abandon all back-issue purchasing (except for extensive runs to extend new subscriptions) while documenting and comparing data on cost versus actual usage. It is expected that costs, including staff time, will not be supported by usage figures. The ideal of providing "perfect" service in the form of a complete periodical file will give way to providing access to needed information through various means.

When issues have been received but lost, promptness will often make the search easier. Recent issues are likely to be available from the publisher, but acquiring them may be a slow process, involving generating a purchase order and possibly prepaying, purchasing an entire volume, and waiting for shipment from overseas.

Beyond the publisher, there are services such as EBSCO's Missing Issues Bank to which customers may contribute duplicate issues and to which they may send want lists free of charge. The recently resurrected Universal Serials and Book Exchange (USBE), if successful, may continue to be the primary source for back issues of serials, especially scholarly journals. It functions as a nonprofit membership organization serving the library community. For a relatively modest fee, a library may become a member, gaining the right to purchase any available back issue for a low price. Members are also expected to contribute duplicates. The focus is on the recent past, Roman alphabet only. If a library is serious about obtaining back issues, USBE can be an economical means of doing so. Other dealers in back issues also supply this market, but complete volumes must sometimes be purchased.

ONLINE MATCHING SERVICES

Automation offers a tantalizing prospect to the out-of-print market. Given the fragmented, disorganized nature of this business and the difficulty of matching items for sale with those who seek them, the promise of a computerized matching service seems attractive indeed.

Currently, the most promising such databases are BookQuest and SerialsQuest, services of the F.W. Faxon Company. Because they have the backing of this large corporation and the benefits of its expertise in programming and marketing, as well as its immense customer base, these services have more than a little hope of success. Each is a database of dealers' available stock and libraries' (or others') want lists. The computer matches the two and alerts users when matches are found. Searching for matches continues each night until the list is removed. Users can also perform direct online searches, including subject searches, for titles they are interested in. Actual sales are handled between dealer and library. There is also a bulletin board feature.

Despite their promise, there are problems with these systems. Given the novelty of this kind of service, dealers are reluctant to input their lists until more potential customers have signed on, and libraries are reluctant to join until more dealers' lists are in. Moreover, many out-of-print dealers do not have their lists in a computer, ready to produce a disk that can be loaded into a database. There also is some duplication of titles, which might tend to drive prices upward. Without authority control, which such a database is unlikely to have, matching may be difficult. There will also be all the usual failures despite apparent matches—wrong edition, different book, no response to order, failure to hold the

SUMMARY

To find a partner among OP dealers:

1. Learn about the OP business.
2. Select dealers with care.
3. Adapt.
4. Give dealers leeway.
5. Maintain personal contact.
6. Have patience!

book for the library, price too high, etc. In Joe Barker's words, "OP listing and searching online may inadvertently become OP hide and seek." There are various costs involved in addition to the purchase price of an item once it is found. There may be a subscriber fee for the database, connect time charges, and transaction charges. This again points to the need for the library to carefully define its goals and to be well organized in its approach.

Obviously, any database of this sort will be most successful when it contains a large variety of material and if it is user friendly. It can be efficient and a great time saver. There were those who said that the computer would have little effect on libraries, and there are those who say there is little future for automated OP searching. Nevertheless, chances are automated matching services are here to stay.

10 THE PRICING PROBLEM

This chapter concerns the problems libraries and vendors face when budgets fail to keep up with rapidly escalating costs for library materials.

Librarians' complaints about excessively high prices and accusations of price gouging have overrun the literature and dominated many meetings over the past decade. Some publishers have responded insensitively, while publishers who tried to cooperate with the library community and its suppliers sometimes felt that their efforts went unappreciated. Vendors, not surprisingly, have found themselves caught in the middle. It is clear that this situation cannot continue indefinitely. Prices are unlikely to reverse their upward trend, nor are library budgets likely to acquire generous proportions in the foreseeable future. Nevertheless, it may be possible to learn from this debate and to proceed in ways that will benefit all concerned.

It may be useful to review the debate over pricing as it has developed over the recent past and to set forth the varying points of view of the participants. It may then be possible to see how pricing issues have affected the vendor/librarian partnership and to suggest some possible courses for the future.

PRICES

The rise in prices of materials purchased by North American libraries can be traced back into the 1970s, but it was in the 1980s that price increases, shrinking budgets, inflation, and a weak dollar caused an outcry from the library community. It became a constant theme at conferences throughout the 1980s, as evidenced by proceedings of such meetings as the Charleston Conference, the primary forum for discussion between librarians and vendors and, to some extent, publishers as well. Topics such as "Today's Primary Issue—Pricing and Costs of Library Materials" were common at these meetings.

It should be noted that North American libraries are not the only ones to suffer from rising costs and meager budgets. Libraries elsewhere, especially in Britain, have suffered budget cuts and rising prices with very much the same effects that have been felt in North America. In a 1987 article in *The Bookseller*, published in London, Peter Mann stated that "whatever problems universities in general have, university libraries have worse ones." In 1989 the same journal carried a piece entitled "University Libraries—A Sad Tale of Decline."

BOOK PRICES

During the 1980s, the price of books increased significantly. Statistics on average book prices are not always directly applicable to library purchases. The type of books purchased, the subjects emphasized, the sources of the books, the country of origin of the books, even the definition of "book," all affect the actual price of the books purchased by any given library. Nevertheless, published figures do indicate overall trends. *Publishers Weekly* regularly publishes statistics on the number of titles and their prices. These figures show that prices more than doubled during the decade. Figures published in *Choice* analyzing prices of over 6,000 college books reviewed in that journal show an average price jump from $18.02 in 1978 to $40.54 in 1989. *Publishers Weekly* figures for hardcover books show a 1977 average price of $19.22 and a 1989 average of $40.24.

Another factor has been a tendency of publishers to adopt fluid pricing for books. Rather than establishing a firm price that is printed on the dust jacket, books may carry no visible price at all. Publishers may simply raise the price whenever it suits them without the annoyance of dust jacket prices in need of correction. Prices listed in *Books in Print* may not be valid. One learns the actual price the publisher is charging when the book is purchased.

Libraries are protected to some extent from unannounced price increases of this sort by the fact that many library order forms state that, if the price is more than a certain amount over the order price, the supplier is to report before shipping. In case of extreme differences, many vendors will report anyway, especially for nonreturnable items. However, the cumulative effect of increases for monographs—whether firm-ordered, received on approval or blanket order plans, or standing order—has certainly impacted library budgets. Book budgets were diminished first by inroads made by expanding serials costs and, second, by the increasing costs of books themselves. Had book prices remained stable after 1978, roughly twice as many books could have been purchased with available funds in 1989 as was actually the case.

Net pricing has come to the fore in recent years as well. This is the practice by which publishers avoid setting a retail price, usually for textbooks and other academic material. They may set both a retail price and a price to be charged to a book store, or they may simply invoice the bookstore and suggest no retail price, leaving that up to the store. This permits bookstores to set prices that give them acceptable profit margins. Perhaps inadvertently, this practice also makes it hard for libraries to know the price of books they wish to buy and it allows vendors considerable latitude in establishing prices.

Trade publishing has seen a decade of takeovers and the paying of huge advances in the hopes of creating yet another bestseller. Rapid acquisition of companies sometimes resulted in lack of careful management. Some big losses have been suffered, and publishers are adjusting by sharpening their practices. Perhaps some will be more selective about what they publish; perhaps initial print runs will be smaller, advances to authors smaller, and marketing more finely honed. Publishing may become the domain of accountants and financiers, not editors. If the publishing industry tightens its belt, the only direction for prices is up.

For many publishers, the library market is a small part of overall sales and receives little direct attention. Those publishers that do sell significantly to libraries are aware of the inroads into monograph publishing that have been made by serials. The natural response to this is to raise prices. As noted in *Publishers Weekly* (July 15, 1989), the scientific, technical, and professional publishing market is expected to grow "from pricing, not unit sales."

Indeed, it has been pointed out that both university presses and scientific publishers for whom the institutional market is the mainstay, have a captive and not very discriminating customer base. Many libraries look on university press books, and science and math imprints, as automatically of higher quality than others. Many of both types are purchased through approval plans. Given this situation, there is tremendous incentive to raise prices.

PRICES OF SERIALS

The most prominent part of the pricing problem has been the cost of subscribing to journals. If a book carries too high a price, one can simply not buy it. Journals subscribed to by libraries through vendors are normally renewed some months before the subscription actually expires, and before prices for the coming year are known. Commitment to unknown prices in normal times of modest price increases met or bettered by budget increases was entirely benign. It was not until the recent concatenation of several costly factors that its inherent danger became evident, and then only after the harm had been done.

Libraries' financial problems with journal pricing made their way out of the professional literature and into such publications as *Science, The New York Times,* and *The Wall Street Journal.* In 1987, *Science* ran a piece entitled "Libraries Stunned by Journal

Price Increases," which focused on the possible cancellation of scientific journals due to rising prices and the then-recent drop in the dollar's value. The following year, *The New York Times* published an article entitled "American Libraries Are in Crisis Over the Cost of Scholarly Journals," describing the efforts of the New York Public Library to realign its serials purchases as a result of escalating costs.

The professional literature abounded with pieces on the problems resulting from the sudden large increase in the price of subscriptions. Although periodicals' prices in general were often the issue, certain publishers received the brunt of the criticism. Not only high prices, but also publishers' differential pricing policies were criticized. Many journals establish one price for individual subscribers and a higher price for institutional subscriptions. In addition, some foreign publishers establish different prices for subscriptions based on the location of the subscriber, with North American subscribers paying substantially higher rates. (Publishers of North American journals do this in reverse.) Publishers explain higher institutional prices by noting that library copies of journals have many readers, while an individual subscription presumably has only one. To equalize prices would mean charging individuals much higher rates. Likewise, pricing by geographical location is explained by citing added costs of doing business in North America, but this fails to explain why such pricing sometimes occurs even when the subscription is purchased through an agent who can pay for many subscriptions with one check in the publishers' preferred currency.

In addition, less visible factors such as the use of acid-free paper, demanded by libraries, and rising foreign labor costs also contribute to publishers' costs and ultimately to increased subscription rates. Other serials obtained on a standing-order basis also showed price increases and are a similarly long-term commitment of libraries. Law libraries and others with significant collections of legal materials noted a sharp increase in the number and cost of updates to loose-leaf legal treatises. Again, cancellation was the obvious recourse, but with a difference. Cancelling a subscription to such updates need not condemn the library to lacking the information permanently. Instead, entire new sets can be purchased at several year intervals, at a considerable savings over constant supplementation. This gives law librarians a more potent tool to use against publishers whom they believe are publishing too fast at inflated prices.

Indeed, the Association of Research Libraries' report on serials prices (1989) may have been the capstone of some years of dissatisfaction on the part of libraries. The report concluded that, in ARL libraries, the median price of purchased serials had increased 32 percent since 1986 and that as a result "more money is being spent to acquire fewer materials resulting in less comprehensive collections." The ultimate effect of this is "deterioration of our research capability in the humanities and social sciences as well as technology and the sciences."

The report made a number of practical recommendations, as well as suggestions relating to seeking alternatives to commercial publishers and to reform of the academic promotion and tenure process and the awarding of grants. Libraries were urged to conduct annual reviews of expensive titles, to study the use patterns of their serials, and to promote greater use of existing serials collections.

The report was critical of commercial publishers, their market dominance, and what was seen as more than sufficient profits. Naturally, this aroused some response from the publishing community. The report was accused of presenting partial and deceptive information and erroneous conclusions. This dichotomy between the libraries' and publishers' views remains unresolved. Nevertheless, libraries have taken and will take action to contain their serials costs no matter how many times publishers attempt to explain away rising subscription prices.

PROLIFERATION OF INFORMATION

Increases in available information have been manifest in several ways, most notably in the field of journal publication. In 1987 *The Wall Street Journal* published an article entitled "Mollusks, Semiotics and Dermatology: Narrow Scholarly Journals Are Spreading," which pointed out that "narrow-interest publications are emerging by the thousands." While poking fun at some of the topics published in these journals, this article, and others like it, also points out the effects on libraries. For example, Harvard's main library added 20 percent to its list of subscriptions in the preceding five years. Moreover, these journals carry price tags right up there with their well-known counterparts. Even if all else remained the same, adding 20 percent to a title list could easily add at least 20 percent to expenditures for subscriptions.

These new journals come in two basic types, the brand-new journal created to publish in a particular field or to direct scholarly attention to a little-known school, and the journal that is an offshoot of an older one. The latter phenomenon, called "twigging," is a reflection of increasing specialization within some traditional fields of study, such as chemistry.

The increase in the number of journals is evident from published figures. For instance, in 1980 *Ulrich's* listed 62,000 periodicals, while the 1990 figure was over 92,000. The *Ulrich's Plus* database shows a total of 68,233 new serials published from 1970 through 1990. Because some records lack starting date information, the actual figure is probably higher, and, of course, some titles ceased as well. Nevertheless, this is a significant flow of new sources of information. An interesting and perhaps encouraging fact to emerge from the data is that the number of new serials per year seems to be declining, with the lowest figure recorded for 1990, when only 621 new titles were listed, compared to 4,090 in 1970 and a high of 4,143 in 1973. Nevertheless, the total output of information is unlikely to diminish, even if new serial titles do decline.

Moreover, existing journals may increase in number of pages published, which raises the subscription price. Naturally, each of these journals claims to be essential, and library clientele very likely will demand that many of them be added to collections. The greatest increase seems to be in scholarly journals, although the more popular types of magazines also proliferate, especially those dealing with such topics as computers. Newly significant topics such as AIDS and environmental health result in increased publication. However, recent information calls into question the necessity to the scholarly community of so many journals. In part fueled by statistical output from the Institute for Scientific Information, debate continues about the value of scholarly output. Studies of citation rates by the Institute indicate that some publications may be little used. Others argue for a greater emphasis on teaching by college and university faculty and less pressure to publish as a means to reduce the flow of publication and ensure that what is published is truly of value. However, little has been done to reduce the flow. A few universities such as the Harvard Medical School have set limits on the number of papers a candidate for review may submit.

Likewise, a steady output of new books appeared, averaging around 31,000 new titles per year between 1980 and 1989. The *Books in Print Plus* database for 1990 included over 840,000 available titles. British publishers produced some 47,000 new books in 1980, compared with 78,000 in 1989.

At the same time, new formats appeared. By 1990 purchases of software, video- and audiocassettes, compact disks, and CD-ROMs were commonplace. None of these items is inexpensive. CD-ROMs, in particular, are often reference material that may duplicate or surpass print titles. Yet they are generally treated as added titles, rather than substitutes for traditional media. Their cost is generally greater than their print counterparts, sometimes considerably so. Increased access to information, such as through rapid, easy-to-use indexes on CD-ROM, causes library patrons to demand these sources.

The University at Albany Libraries did not purchase its first CD-ROMs until 1989. Nevertheless, by the 1990/91 fiscal year, CD-ROM subscriptions were consuming over $120,000 of the acquisitions budget, only a few hundred of which was balanced by cancellation of print titles. This does not include hardware or staff costs. This investment in CD-ROM technology is modest by many libraries' standards.

INFLATION

Although the prices for various commodities may change at different rates, library materials are subject to the same forces that push other prices upward. Increasing costs for the various components that go into producing a book or journal, including raw materials, editorial costs, printing, binding, labor, marketing, and postage in the country or countries where a book or journal is produced, must be reflected in the price charged by the publisher. Inflation may be low in the purchaser's country, but high in the producer's country, distorting the buyer's perception of fair price. As has been pointed out, figures show that for certain types of books, prices essentially doubled between 1977 and 1989. During this period, the Consumer Price Index for commodities other than food rose a total of 64 percent.

WEAK DOLLAR

The dollar's loss of buying power over the past decade has had a profound effect on costs of library materials produced outside the

United States, yet the focus has often been elsewhere in the debate over rising costs. Daily newscasts report the dollar's strength against such currencies as the Japanese yen and the German mark. However, the consequences of the dollar's relative strength or weakness are not obvious unless one makes regular comparisons because this factor merges with other influences on the acquisitions budget to produce on overall effect. A quick look at exchange rates shows what has happened to the dollar in relation to the mark: in June of 1985 the exchange rate was .3240; in January 1991 it was .6464, almost double. This means that every acquisitions dollar spent on German titles went half as far in 1991 as it did in 1985. Vendors may sometimes offer slightly different rates on any given day than *The Wall Street Journal* tables show, but the overall trends are the same. And remember, this statistic ignores price increases and the proliferation of titles. It only shows what has happened to the dollar's buying power.

The *Index Medicus™ Price Study, 1986-1990* clearly shows average prices by subject and country of origin for 2,337 health science journals. Percent of change in average price between 1986 and 1990 varied from 14 percent to 166 percent overall, but it is the country-of-origin table that is most reflective of the effects of the weakened dollar. This table shows that U.S. prices for titles from the Netherlands increased 91 percent, from West Germany 96 percent, and from Japan 145 percent over the period.

LIBRARY BUDGETS

Although most acquisitions librarians believe that their budgets have shrunk in recent years, the fact is that most have increased each year over the previous. For example, the University at Albany Libraries acquisitions budget increased over 67 percent between 1970/71 and 1980/81, and nearly doubled again by 1990/91. This might seem to be reasonable growth, but it could not be stretched to purchase all that libraries needed to buy. Along with others, this library found itself committed to subscriptions, including many foreign titles, that consumed the budget and left little for books. During the same period of time, budgets that had formerly gone for library materials were invaded by fees for various memberships and online access.

THE PRICING BATTLEFRONT

THE LIBRARIANS' ROLE

The 1980s might be called the decade of the pricing battles, so constant and strident were the arguments and accusations about high prices. Librarians have been the whistle blowers, documenting the large increases in materials prices, identifying the worst culprits, attempting to gain understanding and better pricing from publishers. Clearly, any one of the factors discussed above would have negatively impacted the ability of libraries to continue comprehensive collecting. All of them concurring has had a near devastating effect on collections of many types. Out of necessity, fewer books were purchased and serials cancelled, but prices have not reversed their upwards trend, and observers expect them to continue to rise. Librarians issued the call to battle and identified the primary enemy as periodicals publishers who practiced price-gouging tactics. However, publishers and vendors found themselves on the receiving end of pointed questions and criticism.

THE PUBLISHERS' ROLE

Some publishers participated in forums where the issue of price increases was discussed. They presented data to show the myriad costs involved in producing a book or journal, how costly it is to start a journal, how one may lose money for years on a journal and must support it from the profits of other journals. Book publishers pointed to general inflation and the rising cost of such materials as paper. All denied charges of excessive profit-making. As long as libraries continue to buy highly priced materials, including the journals they consider to be the most overpriced, control of the market will remain with the publishers and they will charge what the market will bear.

Publishers are businesses. Their purpose is to make a profit; without it they cannot long survive. When a publisher pays an advance to an author, it is done with the expectation that the book will make a profit for the publisher. No publisher will buy a manuscript that is expected to be a flop just because it has something worthwhile to say. The reverse may happen, however. A book that has little to recommend it may be published if it is expected to sell well. Publishers are not librarians, and there is no reason why they should be expected to think or act like librarians.

VENDOR'S ROLE

Suppliers of library materials found themselves on the pricing battlefield because the prices they charge are based on the price the publishers charge them. Bearing the blame for publishers' actions while they saw their own profit margins diminishing was painful indeed. As early as 1981, vendors were asking publishers for better discounts, but with little satisfaction. Retailers often receive better terms than wholesalers. Thus, vendors may feel that publishers fail to appreciate the role they play in the distribution process.

Far more vendors than publishers met with librarians to discuss pricing problems. They lost business when libraries ordered fewer books, cancelled or cut back approval plans, and cancelled subscriptions. Competition increased among vendors vying for their part of this shrinking market. Some resorted to various ploys to gain or retain business, such as unrealistically high discounts. Along the way, some of these vendors failed, and more will probably follow. If an offer sounds too good to be true, it probably is. Books at unheard-of discounts may net the library a few bargains, but eventually they may also net the vendor a bankruptcy and the library scores of unfilled orders. On the other hand, some vendors have purchased failing companies, expanding their own scope while preventing potential losses to libraries. Pricing crises have spurred some to offer services such as prepayment plans and to assemble and publish data on pricing issues.

Those vendors surviving today find it harder than ever to make a profit. Those who survive into the twenty-first century may well be the largest and the most automated because they will be able to adapt to changing markets.

ONE WORLD

Pricing issues will be affected by the emergence of a global outlook among publishers. Both publishers and vendors are ahead of libraries as participants in globalism. Publishers are forming worldwide companies aimed at a world market. Almost all British books of interest to North American readers are available in North America shortly after, or simultaneous with, their publication in Britain, because their publishers are British/American companies or because of various copublishing agreements.

Likewise, library suppliers may already be British-American, or they may be European companies with North American representatives. They may be well versed in doing business in North America and may have electronic connections across the Atlantic. Other North American vendors have electronic access to the British equivalent of *Books in Print*. Such interconnections will only increase in the years ahead as the European Community becomes established after 1992. Acquisitions librarians and vendors must be aware of developments in the European Community, which will inevitably have an effect on the selling and buying of library materials. Exactly how things will develop and how the shape of the EC will affect libraries remains to be seen. Many details have yet to be settled regarding pricing and taxes. It is expected that, once initial difficulties always attendant on a new enterprise are worked out, the functioning of Europe as one rather than 12 separate economies should benefit libraries that buy foreign materials. Fewer barriers may mean increased competition between vendors trying to compete in a global market.

There may also be more material published in English if European publishers view North America as a promising market. Eastern Europe's role remains a question mark, but this area may eventually become part of the EC and may also view North America as a new market. Such eventualities would add to the pool of available material from which libraries would have to select the most appropriate.

WHERE DO WE GO FROM HERE?

There have actually been some good effects of the pricing wars. In fact, the pricing battlefront has been the impetus for increasing communication between librarians and vendors. The Charleston Conference was first held in 1980, and its attendance has grown each year. It has become the primary forum for discussion of acquisitions issues. This and other forums have permitted a much greater exchange of information than took place formerly and have involved acquisitions librarians in some valuable analysis of publishing, purchasing patterns, and collection use.

In order to gain control of their budgets, librarians are becoming active on several fronts. Study and analysis of the publishing and distribution of the materials libraries buy is an ongoing necessity. Data collection and communication with library administrators and constituencies is critical. New definitions of collection building are unavoidable, as is much more selective purchasing. Continuing efforts to shore up funding and find sources of creative funding will be needed. Underlying all of this is the partnership between libraries and their suppliers, which, if carefully developed and utilized, can play a role in each of the above areas.

RESEARCH: COLLECTING THE DATA

Data gathering and analysis concerning the publishing and supply of library materials are a constant need. This kind of work goes beyond "how we did it" or enumeration of the effects of rising prices and presents information on which decisions may be made or further investigations based. Some recent papers that make use of an analytical approach include St. Clair and Treadwell's "Science and Technology Approval Plans Compared," Betsy Kruger's approval plan study (see Chapter 7 bibliography), and various articles by Christian Boissonnas and Charles Hammaker.

In addition, each library must perform its own analysis because each library is unique. This kind of ongoing data collection and analysis is essential in communicating with other library staff members, administrators, and with a library's users. Awareness of national and world events that affect financial markets as well as data on the Consumer Price Index and exchange rates can permit one to make fairly accurate estimates of future price increases, especially when related to local buying patterns.

Despite the need to collect published data in order to produce a general picture, local data will be the most immediately available and the most pertinent. Published data are generally some months old, whereas local data can be very current. The average price of books published in the U.S. last year is a valuable indicator of general trends, but against that background one may need to show the average price of approval books or firm-orders received during the current fiscal year. With both types of data at hand, discussions of budgetary issues and decision making become much more firmly based.

For ongoing data collection, a binder can be maintained into which are filed photocopies of published statistics of use in making budget requests and spending predictions. This information includes various published book and serial price and title output figures, as well as price projections and analyses from vendors. A table of contents may list the sources from which regular information is expected (i.e., *Publishers Weekly*, *Bowker Annual*, *Library Journal*) and the issue or approximate date when it is expected. These data are photocopied from journals as they arrive in the library and filed in the binder immediately. In addition to statistical information, articles on budget-related issues are kept as well. Only information relating to the most recent years need be kept in the binder. As more recent material accumulates, older material is moved to files. Everything is kept in chronological order and is supplemented by a similar collection of exchange rate tables from *The Wall Street Journal*. Current and retrospective exchange rate data are available from several online services as well as on CD-ROM. A folder of these tables provides ready data for analyses of what the dollar has done and evidence of current trends. Parallel to this, local data are collected on numbers of items and amounts spent in various categories and assembled in monthly reports. Additional local data are available for analysis should the need arise. All or part of such data can be stored and manipulated using a personal computer. This simplifies preparing budget documents, answering questions, and generally keeping abreast of pricing and budget questions.

Libraries with automated acquisitions systems cannot assume that the system will provide the answers to all questions. Programming may be needed, even the use of separate software with downloaded or re-entered data. The expectation that costs will continue to outrun budgets gives libraries an opportunity to make more creative use of funds. Issues relating to costs and budgets provide wide scope for data collection and analysis. Librarians can collect data to show use of the collection and citations of articles in journals being purchased, and thereby present evidence for what material is and is not used. Librarians can be involved in analysis of the need for and uses of online full text. What titles and types of materials are most needed in this mode? Which approval plans, standing orders, subscriptions, vendors are most cost effective? Is the library acquiring the right materials for its clientele? Could available funds be better used by cancelling an approval plan(s) or standing order(s), by changing vendors, by expanding approval plans, by negotiating a different discount schedule with a supplier, by moving certain subscriptions from one vendor to another?

The questions are endless and demanding, but without ongoing data collection and analysis, librarians will be at the mercy of both circumstances and vendors' sales pitches.

It is important to analyze pricing trends by type of material, by discipline, and by country of origin; to correlate prices, purchasing patterns, and usage; and to delineate the effects of methods of purchasing various types of material. Fine tuning collections to clientele is an embryonic art that can be developed through data collection and analysis. Likewise, by doing such research, libraries can gain credibility with administrators, clientele, and vendors. See

Appendix A for a list of sources useful in collecting data on pricing issues.

COLLECTION BUILDING: A NEW DEFINITION

As libraries outgrow both their physical and financial space, a new definition of collection building seems unavoidable. And, as it is realized that control has very nearly been lost, that collections are not what they ought to be, libraries are coming to accept a new reality, a new way of building a collection in part through access to information that is owned and housed elsewhere. Providing what a patron needs when he or she asks for it may supplant the old ideal of anticipating needs by building an encyclopedic collection that will be there ready and waiting when the patron arrives. There is too much information, too little money, and such diverse patron needs that anticipating them is impossible on all but the most basic levels.

Such a redefinition of collection building may take different forms in various types of libraries. It is certainly widely discussed as inevitable among academic libraries, many of which have begun to move in this direction already. Certain libraries may be able to continue building collections, but electronic access to information cannot fail to affect them.

Given the complex of factors that have produced the pricing problem in library materials, respite is unlikely any time soon. In fact, respite may never be forthcoming for academic libraries bearing the brunt of extremely expensive scientific, technical, and medical journals. Instead, some expect the entire system to change, resulting in a radical reorientation of the dissemination of scholarly information. This means not lower prices for journals, but different means of communication, electronic means. Some see the National Research and Education Network, or something like it, linking institutions and individuals nationwide as the means by which such a revolution might be achieved. Such a new means of communication would be supported by new modes of thinking about research, funding, the role of universities, and education.

A rigorously maintained core collection of hard copy and microform materials (possibly augmented by local off-site storage) with an array of electronic media providing access to information on a national and international scale may constitute the library's collection. In this view, a collection is more than a tangible entity housed locally. It is a far-ranging concept that includes much that is not locally owned. This calls into question selection based largely on *Choice* cards or approval slips, many standing orders (especially for monographic series), and "until forbid" subscriptions. How much unneeded and indeed unused material has been purchased and still remains in collections due to such methods of acquisition? And how much more suitable material was not purchased?

RESOURCE SHARING

Resource sharing, which has seldom received much more than lip service, is a realistic way to stretch limited funds. In the past, when money was plentiful, it was easier to buy than to share. Rather than a coordinated effort to build one library's collection in one area while strengthening another library's collection in another area, resource sharing has too often been nothing more than one library loaning items it happens to have to another library that happens to lack them. In implementing resource sharing, it will always be difficult to decide which library will buy which materials with the expectation that they will be used by another library's clientele. It is difficult to accept gaps in the collection and to listen to patron complaints about having to go elsewhere to obtain a needed item.

Resource sharing reduces opportunities for browsing. Even online union catalogs, which combine the holdings of several libraries, are a poor substitute for shelf browsing and assume not only that the system can produce appropriate responses to a user's query and that the user can use the system effectively, but also that the user can effectively identify what he or she needs from the citations in the system alone. There are questions relating to libraries that borrow heavily but lend little or nothing, as well as competitiveness among libraries.

Nevertheless, circumstances are increasing the incentives to develop meaningful programs for the cooperative use of library materials. The University of California has an extensive and successful cooperative program. There is cooperative buying of periodicals at the "Five Colleges" (Amherst, Hampshire, Mt. Holyoke, Smith, and the University of Massachusetts) in central Massachusetts. A library consortium elsewhere in New England is moving toward cooperative cancellation of subscriptions. Instead of hard copy, these libraries will provide current contents online and document delivery from the journal publishers. In New York State an experiment is testing the feasibility of reducing the duplication of subscriptions among the libraries of the four State University of New York university centers, with the subscriber supplying fax copies to patrons of nonsubscribers on request.

Although the degree to which a library moves into a resource-sharing mode will depend on many factors, it seems that interconnectedness and an expanded view of the collection are unavoidable. Electronic media, while broadening use through increased access to data, are also revolutionizing the interlibrary loan process itself. This was signalled by the appearance in 1990 of a new journal, *The Journal of Interlibrary Loan & Information Supply*. There are three significant points about this journal: 1) the recognition of the need for such a journal at this time; 2) the prominence in its pages of information on standards; 3) the inclusion of "information supply" in the title. This journal is about a radical transformation in the transfer of information between libraries.

The development of standards for the interchange of information between systems (referred to in Chapter 2) combined with ever-enhanced technologies has the power to propel interlibrary loan from the still largely manual, slow process it is today to the forefront of library automation. Libraries must summon the vision and administrative skill to make use of these technological developments.

This is not to say that efforts to gain increased funding must cease. Being informed and ready to respond to budgetary questions, librarians will be prepared to make their cases for funding. However, constantly increasing funding, even if it were available, would not alone permit libraries to meet the challenges facing them.

THE PARTNERSHIP

Although the pricing battleground has produced some skirmishes between vendors and librarians, overall it has been an opportunity to develop the partnership. The ongoing nature of issues relating to costs of library materials and best uses of inadequate funds means that libraries and vendors need to work together more than ever.

Librarians must understand the vendor's role, the vendor's pricing structure and the vendor's need to remain profitable. The existence of a variety of reputable, knowledgeable vendors benefits libraries. Libraries can assist the marketplace by encouraging those vendors who provide the best overall service. This means carefully evaluating what a given vendor does for a given library, demanding a fair price, and paying for needed services.

Librarians need to know how vendors arrive at prices and what costs are involved in developing new services, and vendors must be willing to tell them. Ultimately, the price tag for services is una-

SUMMARY

To outwit the pricing crisis:

1. Move beyond complaints.
2. Keep abreast of economic issues affecting libraries.
3. Act to regain control of the budget.
4. Work actively within the organization to realign priorities.

voidable. The questions are: What is worth paying for? What can vendors do better than the library for the cost?

Different libraries will need different kinds of services. Variety among vendors will assure that a particular library's needs can be met, but in order to maintain that variety libraries must select vendors knowledgeably.

Vendors must provide fair prices and good service, participate in the library community, neither practicing nor encouraging in others unethical behavior in order to gain business. They must freely share information, discuss controversial topics, and be willing to state possibly unpopular positions. Although participating in the library community is expensive, it can strengthen the partnership and encourage joint efforts on important issues, as well as increase librarians' knowledge on pricing issues.

As libraries refine collecting policies, vendors need to know what materials libraries will purchase at what prices. Collectively, vendors and librarians can communicate with publishers on pricing and other issues. Vendors with the ability to collect and analyze data on a large scale can produce valuable studies of pricing trends, which libraries can use along with local data.

Continued cooperation on pricing issues is imperative if libraries are to succeed in a changeable and demanding environment and if vendors are to remain viable. This issue highlights how much each needs the other and how interdependent both vendor and library are. For both librarians and vendors, this requires honing the relationship and keeping it one of equals. For both, it means running a carefully managed, no frills operation based on knowledge and evaluation.

11 EVALUATION

A PROFESSIONAL RESPONSIBILITY

Throughout this book, there has been an emphasis on the librarian's need to be informed and critically evaluative. It has been emphasized that initial vendor selection is extremely important and should be done judiciously. That is an evaluative process engaged in prior to experience with a given vendor. This chapter focuses on evaluating vendors with which a library has experience. Ongoing vendor evaluation will provide a solid basis on which to judge untried vendors. It is simply the most important part of the partnership.

There are risks in the merging of library and vendor that only careful evaluation can avoid. Failure to examine the performance of the recipients of large portions of libraries' materials budgets is professionally insupportable and courts the possibility of committing library funds inappropriately. Different types of vendors may be evaluated differently. For instance, suppliers of firm-ordered books, approval plans, out-of-print material, and periodical subscriptions will be judged by somewhat different criteria. Likewise, one library may be satisfied with a particular vendor's service, while another may be unsatisfied. Clearly defined local criteria are the basis from which all evaluation springs.

This is an area in which librarians must tread with great care, designing evaluative tests scrupulously and communicating dissatisfaction, in particular, with tact. Care must be taken in communicating test results with other libraries lest they act upon negative reports that may not apply to them or that may be erroneous or misunderstood. Reputable vendors willingly participate in evaluative studies. A viable relationship will withstand scrutiny, and vendors should have nothing to hide, although they may fear the consequences of poorly conceived studies.

How many libraries have asked vendors to evaluate them? In the interests of professionalism and fostering the partnership between librarians and vendors, librarians should take this kind of critical look at themselves. A library tends to view vendors through the lens of its own procedures and practices with the expectations that vendors will comply with all their requests. Vendors, the recipients of an almost infinite variety of forms and demands, have learned to adjust. Library rigidity has been met with vendor elasticity, but one need not assume that this is inevitable or advisable. Examination of the evaluation process from the perspective of both the library and the vendor may be in order.

TAKING THE VENDOR'S MEASURE

THE STARTING POINT

Where to begin? A four-step process may provide helpful preparation:

1. Understand what the library wants from its suppliers. What is paramount—low price, rapid supply, various supporting services, or some other factor? This kind of introspection can lead one to question and even to reconsider long-held assumptions about what is important. It is the starting point for all vendor evaluation.
2. Read. Considerable published material is available to help you evaluate vendors. Beginning with *Vendor Evaluation: A Selected Annotated Bibliography, 1955-1987* and moving on to a search of *Library Literature*, one can soon gain an awareness of the hows and whys of evaluation, as well as specific studies that have been done and their applicability or adaptability to one's own situation.
3. Understand statistical methods. There are courses and books in this area (see bibliography). Vendors can be assessed in nonstatistical manners, but statistical studies are useful and require some knowledge of methodology if they are to be properly designed.
4. Use the *Guide to Performance Evaluation of Library Materials Vendors* (American Library Assn.). This valuable publication is essential reading before attempting an assessment of library materials suppliers. Focusing on firm-order vendors, it succinctly describes vendor services, a variety of material types, qualitative and quantitative assessment, and procedures. A similar guide to evaluating serials suppliers is being prepared by ALA's Association for Library Collections & Technical Services' Serials Section Acquisitions Committee.

METHODOLOGIES

The way in which data are collected is as important as clear definition of the questions to be asked. Certainly, a simple study asking one or two questions will be easier to manage than one seeking to deal with multiple variables. However, evaluative studies need not be limited to one type of material or to answering only one question. Report writing and spreadsheet software permit the sorting of data in many different ways in order to provide answers to a variety of questions. What one is willing to take on must depend on one's experience, abilities, and available staff. Advances in automated library systems will soon make it possible to analyze vendor performance in much greater detail than is now possible. Performance of serials suppliers would be analyzed at the issue level. Vendor performance will be distinguishable at many parameters—publisher, place of publication, material type, and rush orders. Flexible reporting systems will permit the creation of highly specific and detailed reports of vendor performance.

This will not automatically accomplish all vendor evaluation, but it will provide data seldom now available. The data will need to be analyzed, not merely accepted. They will form a new basis for examining vendor performance, a new basis for discussion with the vendor, and will demand serious response from vendors.

It is important to remember that the purpose of evaluative studies is to fine-tune the library's relationship with its suppliers. Although results of studies may be shared with other libraries and may be published, this is not their primary purpose. The library conducting a study does it for its own sake: to maximize its understanding and utilization of its human and fiscal resources in order to best serve its clientele. One must be able to justify the decision—for example, to obtain certain types of material from a vendor or vendors rather than directly from the publishers, especially if service charges are involved. Many questions of this sort need ready answers whether to satisfy oneself of the rightness of one's decisions or to answer queries from administrators or auditors. Some ways in which vendors may be evaluated are enumerated below, beginning with the least scientific and working up to true data-based studies.

Intuitive Evaluation: Rare is the acquisitions librarian who does not engage in intuitive evaluation. It is not without its value. It can be a general guide to the relative abilities of vendors and can lead one to areas in need of serious study. Some things are difficult, if not impossible, to document. For instance, librarians continue to complain of vendors who cancel too readily or repeatedly send reports such as "claiming with publisher" rather than put some real effort into pursuing problems with publishers. Librarians may feel that they are being overcharged but cannot document the price charged the vendor by the publisher. Nevertheless, this is impressionism, not true vendor assessment, which must be based on carefully collected and analyzed data.

Spotchecking: It is not necessary to compare one vendor with another. One can conduct checks on a vendor's performance in a systematic manner that will give some indication of the vendor's overall performance. For instance, select at random a certain number of invoices per month from vendors and request that they provide a copy of the publisher's invoice to them for that item. Similarly, check a certain number of periodical renewal prices on a vendor's invoice against the prices given in the current issue of the periodical itself. If a problem seems to arise with shipments from certain vendors, but the boxes are opened in a receiving area other than acquisitions, they can be delivered unopened to acquisitions for a test period during which acquisitions personnel can carefully monitor the condition of shipments as they open the boxes themselves. Thus, the origin of the problem can be pinpointed. Acquisitions staff, if they understand that such things are important, can alert supervisors to a great variety of details that might otherwise be passed over. For instance, when invoices are being input manually into an automated system, format and legibility requirements may change. Only the staff members doing the inputting will realize what the problems are. When the University at Albany Libraries automated, it was found that an extra line skipped between titles on the major firm-order vendor's invoices greatly increased accuracy and ease of input. In addition, the vendor showed an order number on one page of the invoice and the title it applied to on the next, causing confusion. The vendor was able to make the minor adjustments to invoice format without difficulty.

Spot checking can be very effective. There is little extra work involved and little opportunity for erroneous results to occur. It is an ideal method for uncovering vendor practices as well as errors. At the University at Albany Libraries, spot checking has revealed, among other things, errors in billing and a longstanding but long-forgotten policy of embedding shipping charges in book prices, no doubt once requested by the library, but no longer relevant. Such checking has been met with full cooperation by the vendors involved.

Formal Data Collection and Analysis: When a more formal study is undertaken in which large amounts of data are collected and analyzed, a clear, rational methodology must form the basis. Knowing what the library's objectives are will provide a solid basis from which to draw the questions to be addressed in the study. If a library is primarily interested in discount, that may be the focus of the study. Or, perhaps the library wishes to compare the service on rush orders of several firm-order vendors. Perhaps the question to be answered is which of several North American and foreign subscription agents best supplies British titles.

No matter what questions are to be addressed, data collection must be governed by two criteria: 1) there must be a sufficiently large body of data gathered to provide statistically meaningful results; and 2) the data must compare like things. In order to gather enough data, the library must have sufficient orders and invoices of the needed type to generate it and enough staff to collect it. Data-collection methods will need to be devised that will not impact severely on daily operations.

Comparison of like categories can be very difficult to achieve. In fact, the truest test is the least possible to conduct: ordering the same books simultaneously from several vendors. Only libraries doing much multiple copy ordering could conduct such a study, and it would complicate its own work routines. Many libraries rarely order enough multiple copies for this kind of study. There are many ways in which faulty selection of data to be compared can falsify the results of a study. For example, a library that habitually orders most trade materials from one vendor while using another for the more difficult materials cannot legitimately compare their performance. The inclusion of rush orders will distort a study. For the same reason, comparisons among libraries are likely to be invalid. For instance, a library that obtains most of its current trade titles on approval plans and firm-orders only more obscure material will see a substantially longer turnaround time on its orders than a library that firm-orders mostly trade titles, even if these two libraries are using the same vendor.

An appropriate time period must be defined for the study. Sufficient time must be allowed to collect needed data (one might wish to correlate this time period to a fiscal year or calendar year), and there must be reasonable starting and ending points.

LIBRARY PREPARATION

Staff members who will be involved in the project should be involved from the moment the idea is conceived. They need to know what is being studied, who is being evaluated, and why. They need to know if and how the study will impact their work day. They need to know what steps may be taken if current practice or a long-used vendor is found wanting. Invariably, they will have useful suggestions and comments. The study will become more meaningful to them, and they will be more likely to participate in it carefully and accurately.

Likewise, the library must be prepared to deal with the collected data. If downloading from or special programming for the library's automated acquisitions system is needed, library systems staff may be involved. If PC based programs are to be used, does the library have the needed software and hardware as well as the expertise to use it? Whatever method of analysis is to be used, is there time and personnel to do it? Will the librarian have institutional support for making policy changes based on results of the study, should the need arise?

LIBRARIES' IMPACT ON VENDOR PERFORMANCE

There are many ways in which a library's practices affect the success rate of its suppliers. For instance, it took several months for my department to learn that overseas letters stamped "Air Mail" in large red letters were in fact being sent, not by the United States mails, but by a bulk mailing service. Orders assumed to have been in vendors' hands within a week were actually taking a month to arrive at their destinations. This upset claiming cycles and obviated the intense effort that had been put into pushing orders through as the end of the fiscal year approached. Had a vendor study been in progress, the length of time it took to receive these books would have been highly distorted. Other mailroom practices can distort receipt dates. Orders "mailed" on the same date may not actually leave the library together, boxes may arrive at the institution simultaneously, only to reach acquisitions on different days. If a library mail room *and* a campus post office (or loading dock), for example, must both be negotiated by incoming and/or outgoing mail, there are many ways for delays and distortions to occur.

Pricing studies are also difficult to conduct accurately, since, as noted in Chapter 5, comparison of price charged to price found in *Books in Print* is frequently invalid because those prices are subject to change; likewise, the list price shown on the invoice may not be the publisher's list price, making discounts based on it misleading.

Poorly verified bibliographic information, missing or incorrect ISBN numbers, and orders mailed to the wrong vendors all affect apparent vendor performance.

The type of material being ordered will also influence the outcome of a study. Even ordering the same books from different vendors at different times can produce skewed results since the publisher may be out of stock at one time and not at the other. Thus, a librarian preparing a vendor study must keep in mind the fact that such factors as these can make it incorrectly appear that a vendor was slow or unable to supply the book. Vendors have very definite ideas about what constitutes a good evaluative study. They can participate in the design of an evaluative study, which could then be applied to a different vendor. Their input can certainly be sought in the development of evaluations in general since it will be beneficial to know what vendors have found unfair in the past.

EVALUATION APPROACHES

FIRM-ORDERS FOR MONOGRAPHS

When it comes to firm-orders, speed of delivery is one of the factors most often evaluated, but vendors may also be evaluated on pricing, accuracy, reporting, ability to handle rush materials, packaging, invoicing, ability to follow the library's special instructions, adherence to contractual obligations, and various services. The ALA *Guide* provides specific questions to be asked in evaluating vendors, but each library must decide for itself whether these or other factors are significant to it. For instance, the *Guide* includes accurate, complete bibliographic information conforming to cataloging standards as a point of evaluation of invoices and reports. A library with an automated system may only need a rapid access point, probably an order number, and enough bibliographic information to identify the item.

APPROVALS

Why does the library use any given approval plan? Is it expected to provide the library with certain materials rapidly? Is it expected to provide a large percentage of new publications in a specified subject area or areas? Or are there other foci of importance to the library? Expectations of approval plans vary, even within a library, and must be clearly defined before evaluation can begin. Evaluation may be aimed not so much at comparisons among vendors as at delineating exactly what a given plan is accomplishing or failing to accomplish. Approval plans are long-term commitments, like serial orders, and not easily moved among vendors. This makes initial choice very important, but evaluating a plan that has been in place for some time can enable you to point out problems that the vendor should be told about (for example, excessive duplication). It can also clarify the success and range of the plan's coverage in terms of overall collection development policies. Approval plans can also be compared to firm-ordering in terms of discount and staff costs.

As with many things, this is easier said than done. An approval plan is a tricky thing to pin down, meshing as it does with other acquisitions operations and often carrying political baggage as well. Evaluation of current and potential suppliers of a particular approval plan may point to the failure of the current supplier. Acquisitions may have strong reasons to change—the vendor may invoice poorly, duplicate frequently, fail to follow library instructions—yet the bibliographer for that subject may refuse to change. So much inertia may exist within the department and/or elsewhere in the library that changing vendors is virtually impossible. Nevertheless, some gauge needs to be taken of the success of existing plans. A library should know what any given plan is doing for it in terms of obtaining desired materials, at what cost, how use of the plan compares to firm-ordering, how much staff time goes into maintaining the plan, etc.

A plan can be measured simply against library expectations of it in order to determine to what degree the book supplied meets the profile's subject categories, its exclusions, its price limits, the timeliness of receipts, regularity of shipments, amount of duplication, return rates, responsiveness of vendor personnel to library complaints, and the like. The library can then pursue areas of concern with the vendor and determine for itself if the vendor meets expectations sufficiently well to justify continuing the plan.

Approval plans can also be compared to other measures. Comparisons of subject coverage among several vendors can be revealing. Books supplied from several vendors can be analyzed to produce comparisons among the performances. Or books supplied on approval plans can be compared to the universe of publishing. St. Clair and Treadwell's article on a study of this type, referred to in Chapter 7, is a model of this kind of study. In this way a library can determine how much a plan is able to supply of all potential materials. It may indicate that the library is relying on an approval plan to supply materials that in fact is not being supplied. The library may wish to change vendors or to alter firm-ordering policies in order to more adequately supplement the plan.

It is also possible to compare an approval plan with selection by bibliographers in an attempt to determine which materials, over a given period of time, were or would have been obtained by each method. Discounts can be compared as well between approval plans and firm-orders.

In all of this, the primary challenge is to devise a test that is valid. Vendors will cooperate in various ways—for example, by supplying forms for a test period, but there are limits to what can fairly be asked of them. When the University at Albany Libraries attempted to verify the commonly held belief that approval plans carry higher discounts than would be obtained if the books were firm-ordered (see Chapter 7), it was discovered that there were two choices: either compare the stated discount rate on the North American approval plan with the average overall discount given for the past year by the major North American firm-order vendor or get an individual price quote on a sample of approval titles from the firm-order vendor. The former method, its simplicity and its clear answer (1 percent higher discount on firm-ordered books) made it appealing, but it was too crude. Since different types of books are firm-ordered precisely because they do not come on the approval plan, like orders could not be compared. In the latter method, the firm-order vendor would not allow a large enough sample to be definitive. This was understandable given the work load involved. However, a sample of 51 titles was sent to this vendor and exact price quotes received. For these books, firm-ordering would have resulted in a discount 2 percent higher than the approval plan. For two books, there appeared to be problems or errors in the price quote since the percent of discount could not account for the price quoted by the firm-order vendor, but for the remainder both appeared to work from the same list price. This exercise illustrates some of the difficulties inherent in evaluating even an apparently quantifiable figure such as price: the difficulty in comparing like items and in acquiring sufficient data, and problems in evaluating the data.

OUT OF PRINT

Perhaps more than any other area, the success of OP dealers relates to library practices, and their evaluation can easily be misleading. If a dealer is willing to work with the library and provides some success on searches, will hold books awaiting a purchase order, charges acceptable prices, and follows library instructions about shipping and billing, the dealer may be deemed successful. It is possible to keep statistics on the fill rate of out-of-print orders. One may learn that over the course of two years bookseller A supplied 25 percent of the orders received while bookseller B filled 30 percent. If bookseller C supplied 0 percent, the library may want to examine why. Did the library send a small group of orders for chemistry material to a humanities bookstore? Did the library make so many demands that the bookseller was not interested in doing business with it? If few out-of-print orders are placed by the library, statistically significant numbers will not be available. Testing several dealers on sample groups of orders has little meaning. Nor is there any point in constructing a test by sending the same order to several dealers. They may compete against each for the title, driving the price upward.

If a library's out-of-print orders consist mostly of recent, nontrade OP material, the success rate will necessarily be low. Targeting orders to booksellers who specialize in the type of material the library is seeking may help. Dealers who focus on university presses, scholarly material, and art books will be most successful at obtaining those materials, but it takes time for books to reach the OP market. Understanding the dynamics of the out-of-print market will help the library to successfully evaluate its OP dealers and itself in relation to them.

What matters is ultimate success and the quality of the relationship, not the number of days taken on a particular sample. This is a subjective judgment, based on the quality of the relationship that exists between library and book dealer. Libraries habitually seeking esoteric material that are patient and willing to pay and that have secured the confidence of a book dealer have a successful relationship and will give such a dealer high marks.

There is more potential for testing the usefulness of online matching services. Here, one must determine whether the fee paid for the service is justified by the success rate. By tracking the success rate for items sought through an online service, the cost per successfully obtained title can be determined. Comparing the success rate with the success rate of other means the library uses for obtaining out-of-print material will indicate which works better for the library. Much will depend on what kinds of material the library seeks, how large the database is, and how well it is maintained. Ultimately, it will be up to the library to decide whether the cost per title of using an online service is acceptable.

SERIALS: PERIODICALS AND CONTINUATIONS

If acquisitions librarians in general are hard-pressed to deal with vendor evaluation, serials librarians find it nearly impossible.

Because of the long-term commitment to a periodicals vendor and the complexity of moving subscriptions, there may be little incentive to evaluate. The task is not made any easier by the fact that service is such a prime factor in the provision of serials. Nevertheless, some kind of evaluation should occur. The process of correcting a tape-loaded annual renewal invoice, described in Chapter 4, was certainly evaluative. It did not begin as a vendor study, but data resulted that could be used to calculate types and numbers of errors as percentages of the number of titles billed. Even without such analysis of the errors resulting from this renewal, a definite impression was formed. An annual renewal invoice for a periodicals list is an ideal vehicle for evaluation, containing as it does so much concentrated information. Invoice prices can be compared to those listed in the publications themselves. Data can be kept on claims, length of time taken to start new orders, problems and their resolution, and responsiveness of service personnel.

Nevertheless, more systematic studies are invaluable in confirming or disproving impressions and in spotchecking. There is, unfortunately, minimal help available for those who set out to evaluate serials suppliers. The ALA *Guide*, although restricted to firm-order vendor studies, can serve as a starting point when one begins to think about evaluating serials suppliers. The best published article on how to evaluate serials vendors (and it excludes periodicals, newspaper, and services), is Sharon Bonk's *Toward a Methodology of Evaluating Serials Vendors*.

WHAT VENDORS THINK

It should come as no surprise that vendors often look askance at library vendor studies. Knowing that flawed studies have actually caused libraries to take business away from vendors and naturally believing themselves to be deserving of high praise, vendors are sensitive to evaluations of their services. Vendors are particularly wary of studies that they feel make unfair comparisons. For instance, a comparison of timeliness between vendors, one of which provides pre-publication announcements and one which provides slips on publication, is not comparing like situations. On the other hand, it certainly behooves a vendor to take negative results seriously. One must sometimes admit to deficiencies and attempt to remedy them. Then evaluation, especially negative impacts of evaluation, can have positive effects on the partnership, and overall library/vendor relationships should improve. The key here is the formulation of fair and rational studies, the results of which are disseminated with care, with vendors fully informed and given an opportunity to respond.

The question of whether to name vendors or to hide their identity continues to plague both librarians and vendors. Vendor names are usually removed from published evaluative studies, but often bandied around in conversation. It clearly reduces the value of a study to hide the identity of vendors who were evaluated. On the other hand, considerable damage can be done, erroneously, by widespread knowledge of vendors who are rated poorly. Such rating should not cause librarians to cancel orders or stop using given vendors, but they seem to have had this effect. Instead, they should cause librarians to conduct their own studies to validate the findings for their own libraries before even taking a step in the direction of changing vendors. This is a question that merges the practical and the ethical and deserves attention from thoughtful acquisitions people.

Nevertheless, vendors willingly participate in studies as partners of libraries in joint studies and provide reports, extra copies of invoices, and copies of publishers' invoices. This kind of collaborative study can produce interesting and valuable results.

EVALUATIVE STUDIES

Examination of actual evaluative studies is essential before beginning one's own. It is useful to focus not only on the results, but also on the methods used and the way in which conclusions were drawn.

A SIMPLE ONE-QUESTION STUDY

The University at Albany Libraries are currently involved in a study testing the validity of the frequently heard assertion that list price for periodicals does not vary from vendor to vendor. The price paid by this university will be compared to the price paid by another university for a list of titles obtained from different vendors. Service charges will be excluded. Price data will be derived from each library's automated system, with care being taken to obtain for periodicals complete prices, including supplemental charges, and to eliminate any credits applied. At the present time the study includes periodicals and monographic series on standing order.

This study could be replicated many times in numerous permutations. It could also incorporate receipt dates and other factors indicative of overall service. In this case, however, the comparison was limited to price, largely because of the ease with which these data could be obtained and compared and the fact that at one institution significant backlogs of material to be checked in would have invalidated receipt dates.

A MULTIPLE-QUESTION STUDY

The University of California at Berkeley undertook a major vendor evaluation study to answer seven specific questions regarding vendors' ability to supply various types of firm-orders. In all, 21 vendors and approximately 5,000 orders were included in the study. Price was not examined—only the vendors' ability to supply and the speed and quality of fulfillment.

Despite its size, this study was designed to disrupt staff routines and/or add to work loads minimally. Rather than doing random samples of orders already received, all outgoing orders included in the study were randomly assigned to vendors. The orders were first carefully screened and coded as to type (in *BIP*, not in *BIP*, etc.); at least 100 orders in any given category were needed in order to give acceptable results. When items were ready to be ordered, they were "dealt" blindly into pigeon holes created for the vendors under study without being examined. As stated by Joe Barker: "The methodology devised involves randomly assigning vendors within strictly controlled test groups, and later downloading the order records for statistical analysis on another computer."

Analysis of the data provided Berkeley with new insights into their vendors' abilities. Some results were unexpected, such as the high speed of fulfillment from a vendor who was believed to be slow.

The relevance of the questions asked, the careful and straightforward methodology, and the care with which conclusions were drawn make this a study to be emulated and replicated. Its conclusions cannot be accepted as valid for other libraries, but it is precisely the kind of study libraries need to undertake in order to refine their relationships with vendors. Even at Berkeley, the study will need to be repeated as the library's and vendors' circumstances and capabilities evolve. To quote Joe Barker once more: "it is probable that vendors' potential to conform to libraries' needs will take directions we cannot yet even foresee, and the need to evaluate will never cease."

This study should be read and reread in its entirety. See Joe Barker's "Random Vendor Assignment in Vendor Performance Evaluation" listed in the bibliography for this chapter.

COMPARING APPROVAL PLAN VENDORS

Evaluation of approval plan vendors is difficult at best, and impossible if a library has only one plan, unless plans are compared between libraries or unless special arrangements are made with several vendors to supply lists or slips under identical profiles.

In the case of a study conducted at Texas A&M University, the latter method was chosen. Investigators sought to determine if there were any significant differences among two general and two sci-tech specialists' ability to service a sci-tech approval plan. They examined numbers of books supplied and whether the vendors under study supplied the same or different titles. Profiles were developed that were as much alike as possible given the various vendors' different profiling methods. A database was established using dBASE III.

The results of this relatively straightforward study indicated that there was great variation among the vendors in terms of which books were supplied, and that the vendor used for a sci-tech approval plan "makes an enormous difference."

This is also an excellent study to be repeated elsewhere with variations to determine appropriateness of vendors as suppliers of particular types of approval plans. See Gloriana St. Clair and Jane Treadwell's paper "Science and Technology Approval Plans Compared" listed in the Chapter 7 bibliography.

EVALUATING THE LIBRARY

Undertaking the evaluation of a vendor or vendors provides an ideal opportunity for introspection. The careful definition of those factors to be evaluated naturally leads one into the examination of library practices and policies. One explores areas, such as mail room activities that may not otherwise receive regular consideration. Understanding that library practices can affect vendor studies as well as ultimate library costs leads one to question the necessity of longstanding library practices. Most libraries demand that a copy of the order form be returned in the book. Is this really necessary? Certainly it provides immediate identification of the order, including the order number, but the invoice may suffice if it too contains order numbers. On the other hand, in an automated system that provides access by ISBN, that number, prominent in most books, may provide even faster access to an order record. When judging reporting, one will naturally want information to be timely and readily linked with the order record. This may not mean full bibliographic information, but it may mean inclusion of the order number and/or ISBN.

More systematic evaluation of library practices can also be undertaken. Questionnaires can be devised that solicit vendor opinion about library practices, forms, special requests, accuracy and usefulness of information supplied on orders, satisfaction with title mix, and problems encountered in dealing with library staff. This can be somewhat awkward for a vendor who may be reluctant to express negative comments about a customer, especially if there is much that the vendor dislikes or if the relationship is already strained; but with some tact, vendors can be honest. It is indeed enlightening to "see ourselves as others see us" and to consider the impact of library practices on vendors and their services. In a partnership, evaluation must work both ways.

It is also worth exploring what benefits might accrue to a library if it could simplify its requirements enough to have a positive impact on the vendor. If the library saves the vendor money, should not some benefit return to the library, such as a higher discount rate? Working together in this way, to their mutual advantage, the library and the vendor will experience the partnership at its most productive.

THE PARTNERSHIP

The vendor/librarian partnership is a relationship that is built over time. By carefully evaluating vendors at the time of initial selection, librarians increase the likelihood that a fruitful partnership will develop, but there is no assurance that such will be the case. Only by working together for a period of time, paying attention to the relationship, and learning through experience that each is deserving of trust and respect can a worthwhile partnership come into being.

Evaluation will always be necessary because change is a constant in the process of acquiring library materials. Library staffs, procedures, and goals change. Vendor staffs, abilities, and quality of order fulfillment change. The nature of library collections is

SUMMARY
Evaluate, evaluate, evaluate:

1. Develop criteria.
2. Evaluate before vendor selection.
3. Evaluate on an ongoing basis.
4. Analyze data; avoid impressionistic evaluation.
5. Consider library practices from vendor's viewpoint.
6. Communicate.

undergoing rapid change, and consequently, what libraries want from vendors and the service vendors can offer will change. Once an evaluative study has been completed, the only sure thing about it is that it will have to be done again.

This is not a bad thing. It will refine the relationship and assure that the partners understand each other, that the library has chosen its partners wisely, and that the vendors who serve best will receive the business they deserve.

Such rationally evaluated partnerships should encourage the continued existence of enlightened vendors who truly want to be the partners of libraries. In the words of John Berry, editor-in-chief of *Library Journal* (see Chapter 5 bibliography), such enlightened vendors "enhance our professional practice and help us gain wider public acceptance for change, [while] they also create their own opportunities to make a profit." This is what the partnership is all about.

COMMUNICATION

Vendors want honest communication from customers. If a librarian feels that errors and other problems cannot be openly discussed and silently suffers feelings of dissatisfaction, eventually severing the relationship, both vendor and library are hurt. Open discussion might resolve problems before they escalate and before hard feelings develop, may prevent the inconvenience and expense of severing ties with a vendor, and could lead to the development of a mutually beneficial partnership.

12 A QUESTION OF ETHICS

Numerous ethical issues confront the library profession: questions of privacy, censorship, social responsibility, freedom of access, electronic publishing, and copyright, to name a few. As a profession, librarianship is seldom accused of questionable ethics and seems little given to examination of the issue itself. As Lindsey and Prentice point out:

> Codes of ethics, or even official statements on the part of library associations, have not been burning professional issues during the several centuries of American librarianship.

However, the American Library Association does maintain a Professional Ethics Committee and has issued a Code of Ethics, last revised in 1981. The Code deals primarily with the librarian's relationship to library users and the provision of fair, equal, and accurate service. There is little here that is applicable to acquisitions, other than general behavioral attitudes and the expectation that librarians will avoid personal gain at the expense of others. Nor is there any enforcement mechanism as there is in the British code. It is a topic that may need to be pursued with some vigor by the Association for Library Collections and Technical Services in order to direct attention more specifically to acquisitions and other technical service areas.

There are areas, in the acquisition of library materials where some real thought must be given to ethical standards. Indeed, the growing partnership between vendors and librarians has caused new ethical questions to arise. Webster's Third New International Dictionary defines ethics as "the principles of conduct governing an individual or a profession: standards of behavior." Everyone has his or her internalized ethical system, but this alone is not an adequate guide for professional behavior. There must be standards of behavior expected of the profession as a whole, especially in areas where such standards may differ from personal beliefs. If individual ethical systems vary, our perception of what is acceptable professionally will vary as well, and the ALA statement offers no specific guidance. Nor do we find ethics among the course offerings of this country's library schools.

In a time of confused moral values, how does a profession establish and enforce an ethical system for its members? Where do we begin? Professional literature is not totally devoid of material dealing with ethics. Likewise, the literature of other professions may yield thought-provoking material. Some knowledge of business ethics is not an unrealistic expectation since business dealings are at the heart of acquisitions.

Lindsey and Prentice, in a chapter entitled "Cases and Questions," include numerous questions dealing with situations that involve ethical judgments. Some of these questions relate to acquisitions and relationships with vendors, including both librarian and vendor actions in bid situations, differences between business ethics and librarians' ethics, if any, and use of budget lines for other than their intended purposes, as well as more general questions. There are situations described here that will make even the most ethical among us think twice.

A recent publication in this area, *Legal and Ethical Issues in Acquisitions*, presents a variety of thought-provoking topics, from antitrust issues to advertising, libraries and gifts, software issues, contracts, and claiming of periodicals.

While such publications provide food for thought, they offer little that is prescriptive. Librarians must think their way through ethical questions they may face on the job. For acquisitions librarians, this means putting themselves into the shoes of the vendor in order to imagine the effects of certain behavior. Here the focus is not so much on blatant unethical conduct as on more subtle ways in which both librarians and vendors treat each other.

ETHICS AND THE VENDOR

One continues to hear disturbing tales of vendor practices: those who lose or report out-of-print books they do not care to supply at the guaranteed discount; vendors who cancel orders rather than pursue what are in fact problems such as erroneous reports from publishers; the practice of inflating list prices before applying discounts; lack of response to claims; failure to supply at contracted discount rate.

A vendor wishing to obtain orders from a library may try too hard, badgering librarians with numerous phone calls. This is annoying at the very least and likely to be counterproductive as well, but is it unethical? If the vendor goes so far as to circumvent the person whom he has been pestering unsuccessfully and finds another, perhaps the one who actually assigns vendors to orders, and begins a campaign with that person, this seems to go beyond acceptable behavior.

Vendors should be able to explain their pricing policies clearly. They should be willing to provide copies of the publisher's invoice to them and explain how the price billed to the library was computed. A similar explanation of list price and service charge should be forthcoming from subscription agents. Exchange rates should be clearly stated.

It behooves the library and the profession not to tell tales of one vendor to another. Indeed, most reputable vendors refrain from doing so themselves and do not encourage it from customers.

Vendors should be expected to present an accurate picture of their financial condition to their customers rather than suddenly going bankrupt, refusing to respond to communication, refusing to return outstanding orders, and then reappearing under a new guise. Out-of-print dealers, too, have obligations to maintain sound business practices, to charge fair prices, and to accurately describe the condition of the books they offer.

One might cite "exceptional ethical" behavior on the part of vendors. The community service gestures that many companies engage in can certainly be found among library materials vendors, including support of awards and donations of books. Vendors are often willing to carry accounts for libraries whose institutions freeze or delay their budgets, and few inflict interest charges on late payment. In fact, New York State law requires interest to be paid on payments made later than 45 days after receipt of goods and invoice. All major library materials vendors have either returned, refunded, or issued credit for such interest payments made on behalf of the University at Albany Libraries. Are such occurrences "super-ethical" or are they simply good business practice?

ETHICS AND THE LIBRARIAN

One librarian who has worked in acquisitions and collection development and has worked on the vendor side as well claims to have seen as much if not more unethical behavior on the part of librarians than on the part of vendors.

One vendor described being unwittingly involved in a test by a library whose business they had sought for some time. When a few orders were received, the vendor put much effort into them, believing he was building a new relationship. However, after a certain period of time, those orders that remained unfilled were cancelled without explanation and no more were received. Only later did the vendor indirectly discover that the library had simply been engaging in research. The vendor felt he had been misled and used and that the librarian's behavior had been unethical. Further, the vendor would have supplied the information the librarian sought to obtain through these orders if it had simply been requested. Very likely, the librarian would be surprised to learn of this reaction.

Librarians have summarily cancelled entire subscription lists without explanation within weeks of indicating to the vendor that their service was excellent and there were no problems in the relationship. If there are problems, let us discuss them in a professional manner. If administrators force acquisitions librarians to move lists or use certain vendors, acquisitions librarians have another kind of battle on their hands. Mere acquiescence is unprofessional. If the acquisitions librarian is indeed powerless in such a situation, the least he or she can do is to communicate honestly with the vendor.

Approval plans have been suddenly cancelled as well and then, to add insult to injury, large quantities of books shipped during the weeks prior to cancellation of the plan were returned. What does the librarian expect the vendor to do with these books that have been purchased from the publishers for that library's approval plan? Maybe some will be sold, but in the meantime they must be processed and warehoused. Such behavior without explanation or apology is a poor reflection on the profession.

Vendors have a right to serious, businesslike treatment by librarians. Yet how many librarians exhibit any understanding of business practices? Librarians who demand high discounts with no understanding of how discount must be computed or how much money a company must make in order to survive, librarians who demand more and more services "free" are not only ignorant, they are treating their vendors in an insulting and unethical manner.

And what of librarians who encourage vendors to vie for their business by shopping for best discount or by promising large numbers of orders to a vendor who in turn promises no services charges? This only escalates hyperbole and obscures the truth. Carelessness can become unethical behavior or can encourage it in vendors. Knowledge and an awareness of ethical considerations will help librarians stop deceptive sales pitches by making themselves immune.

Librarians often take one vendor's lists or forms (supplied free of charge) and order the material elsewhere. The vendor who supplied the forms is entitled at least to some honest communication. A vendor who provides forms or lists customized to fit a profile developed by the library will certainly expect to receive orders as a result.

In other cases, if vendors are supplying a wide spectrum of new title notifications and they know that the library gets similar notifications from a number of vendors, they may have lower expectations regarding the numbers of orders that will result. Receiving numerous overlapping forms from many vendors seems wasteful at the very least. It is unreasonable to expect vendors to supply such forms year in and year out if no or few orders result. In any case, vendor and librarian should understand each other's view of new title notifications from the outset in order to avoid misunderstandings later.

Vendor evaluations are often a cause of friction between library and vendor. Evaluative judgments are not infrequently made on the basis of intangibles, rather than firm evidence. Even when data are kept and analyzed by the library, vendors may feel that it misrepresents their service. Sometimes vendors simply refuse to accept the truth—that they have failed to keep a customer happy. There is a subtle balance to be achieved here. The vendor must be given fair treatment while the library preserves it prerogative to choose its suppliers freely. Evaluative studies should be conducted on a rational basis and kept confidential, and vendors should be given an opportunity to mend their ways when found wanting.

As for the question of whether to publicly name vendors in discussions of ability and service: Are there certain situations or forums where naming names is acceptable and others where it is not? Vendor names have been edited out of a librarian's article, to the detriment of the article. Some librarians freely name names in conversation, some do not. What about electronic mail? Misinterpretation in any forum is a constant problem. Surely all have a responsibility to set forth their positions clearly, just as listeners and readers have a responsibility to receive the message with care. Is it ethical to act on the basis of another's negative comment? Suppose the comment has been misinterpreted? If vendors are named in an evaluative context, do they not have a right to know what is being said about them? What form does an ethical response from them take?

What is an ethical approach to claiming? Flooding a supplier with automated claims, many of which are erroneous, seems more than simply wasteful. Picture a small out-of-print dealer who receives repeated claims spewed out by an automated acquisitions system. Responding is costly and, with out-of-print searching, is largely meaningless as well. Conversely, is it ethical for suppliers to ignore claims because there are too many of them?

Does any library actually claim journal issues that have been received but subsequently lost? Publishers believe that this is done.

There has been some discussion recently of the acceptability of libraries' accepting donated subscriptions. Aside from the many practical difficulties involved, accepting a subscription paid for by an individual at the individual rate but given to the institution is questionably ethical.

Is it ethical to cancel journals published by a specific publisher in order to support union action against that publisher? Such action would deprive library clientele of access to the information contained in those journals, amounting to censorship. What is an ethical means of disposing of duplicates? Trash them, give them away, send them to a clearinghouse, recycle them, return them to the publisher?

If acquisitions librarians have a service ethic, it must be to provide information where it is needed as quickly and cost-effectively as possible. Suppose that, through no fault of the library, payment for an expensive, badly needed CD-ROM service has been held up through a series of unusual events. The librarian has traced the paperwork, doing all in his or her power to keep it moving through the bureaucracy. The vendor has waited for several months and now states that no more updates will be shipped until payment is received. Does the acquisitions librarian's commitment to getting material to those who need it compel him or her to assure the supplier that the check is on its way (when it is not)—in short, promise anything in order to get the supplier to continue servicing the subscription? Or does the librarian apologize for the failure to issue payment and accept a delay in shipment as the supplier's right?

All general vendors want a good mix of orders—that is, a broad spectrum of high- and low-discount items and easily obtained titles as well as some problem material. They may wish heavy emphasis in whatever areas they specialize in. If vendors are not to be given such a mix, it seems only reasonable to so inform them. Likewise, if a vendor is being used on a trial basis or exclusively for special funds, there is no justification for not making this clear. Where price is a primary concern, high discounts will be sought for easily obtained items, while difficult items may go to vendors who excel in service rather than discount. Neither vendor will get a good mix and they should not be led to believe that they will. All such situations should be explained to vendors, who then have the opportunity to refuse the business. On the other side of the coin, should one vendor give widely differing discounts to similar accounts?

The free lunch, or dinner, the receptions and shuttle buses at conventions, are provided by vendors openly and with no overt demands for special consideration. Such activities are accepted within the profession. Most vendors have little difficulty with the concept of the free lunch, being business people for whom this is simply a part of the American way of doing business. Some are sensitive to hesitancy on the part of some customers to accept such perks. One vendor has even questioned the ethical position of a librarian who refuses a free lunch since the refusal seems to imply that the librarian thinks the vendor is trying to "buy" that library's business, thus impugning the integrity of the vendor. They are also likely to rankle a bit at the librarians who invite themselves out to expensive meals on the vendors' credit cards. But in moderation, a lunch or dinner on occasion provided to customers is seen as harmless, neither an attempt to "buy" the library nor a librarian taking advantage of the vendor, but simply an opportunity to get together for informal discussion and to thank a customer for business received. However, the widely held belief that acquisitions/collection development people can eat their way through ALA meetings, spending virtually nothing on meals, is disturbing. Even worse is the librarian who expects, or even demands, that a visiting vendor representative provide a free lunch. The vendors' "can you top this" approach to extravagant offerings during the ALA annual meeting is less worrisome than the librarians' reaction to them as expected, even due. One of the more memorable moments of the 1986 meeting in New York was the undignified mad dash of librarians to get on a vendor-sponsored boat for a free supper and harbor cruise, crowned by the boat's return to the dock to pick up late arrivals.

Cargill and Alley in *Practical Approval Plan Management* (see Chapter 7 bibliography) take a rather sanguine approach to the vendor paying expenses for a plant visit by a customer, saying that "you are now a customer and this is part of the cost of doing business. You are not being entertained, you are attempting to join with your vendor in good faith to resolve common business problems." They advise against letting the vendor pick up the tab before the librarian is actually a customer, saying, "There's a difference." How much difference there is can certainly be debated, and there are those who would disagree with both of these points.

These things are not free. We, the customers pay, one way or another. Our institutions pay when books are purchased. Librarians may pay personally if their professional judgment is impaired by the memory of a boat trip or a lavish party.

Do acquisitions librarians have an ethical obligation to pay compliments where they are due, when a company does something well or an employee provides exceptional service?

On a slightly different note, as vendor services have proliferated, vendors have often offered and some librarians have demanded that these services be provided free of charge—a report here, a diskette of data there, maybe a little software program thrown in as well. None of this is free either. Most of it is backed by considerable costs on the vendor's part. Expecting such things to be supplied free is, at best, naive. It is far more equitable for all the vendor's customers if such services are offered with a price tag, which can be paid by those who truly desire the service.

Earlier ALA codes expected the librarian to know and perform in accord with the policies of the organization of which he or she was a part. Acquisitions librarians may feel that the regulations of the bureaucracies of which their libraries are a part are damaging to those libraries and prevent them from best serving the library and its clientele. While librarians may (and should) work to change such regulations, what do they do while the regulations remain in effect? Does the fact they are perceived to be inimical to the librarian's professional duty justify finding ways around them?

Another area worthy of some thought is the effect of librarians who move between vendors and libraries during their careers. Will an acquisitions librarian who formerly worked for a vendor favor that vendor excessively when buying materials? Will a trail of shifted periodicals lists be left behind by a former subscription agent turned serials librarian? If so, did the institutions gain or lose as a result of changing periodicals suppliers? Such changes might have been made solely on the basis of loyalty to the previous employer, but they might also reflect superior knowledge of that supplier's abilities. If this were to happen, it would be difficult to determine whether anything unethical had occurred, or even whether the institution gained or lost.

And what about friendships formed? Close personal alliances between librarians and employees of vendors can result in subtle influences and loyalties. This is very much a topic for introspection by those librarians who choose to work on both sides of the fence at different times in their careers.

What does a library owe a vendor who is being dropped or who will receive a marked decrease in business simply because the library has decided to give another vendor a try? A large, unexpected reduction in ordering can have a serious impact on a business. Does the library owe that vendor an explanation, a warning?

What would the library expect of the vendor if the library, with perhaps $60,000 worth of outstanding orders with that vendor, suddenly lost all funding? Would it be ethical for the library to ask that the vendor supply the books and wait until the new fiscal year for payment?

If a library is covered by a statewide contract with stated discounts, is it ethical for it to negotiate its own, better, rate?

If a library negotiates a flat discount rate in return for a certain volume and mix of orders, it is certainly unethical not to provide that volume and mix.

THE BOTTOM LINE

ETHICS AND THE PARTNERSHIP

The preceding discussion should leave no doubt that there are plentiful opportunities for acquisitions librarians to confront ethical issues. It may be difficult, however, to find good working models for guidance, or people who are willing to debate these issues. This is where the partnership becomes important as well as the determination of each partner to behave in an ethical manner.

Researchers Amar Bhide and Howard H. Stevenson found that there are no compelling economic reasons for honesty in business. On the contrary, unethical behavior often *does* pay. Nevertheless, most business people they interviewed believed in honesty. They were, and are, guided not by the profit motive, but by "moral and social motives." In fact, they conclude: "It is the very absence of predictable financial reward that makes honesty a moral quality we hold dear." This makes for a society of optimism and trust, where one thinks the best of someone else until proven wrong and where second chances are possible.

It is also clear that business people adapt to the environment in which they conduct business. If the librarian/vendor relationship is viewed in this light, one can see that ethical behavior on the part of either partner will foster it in the other. Just as businesses operating in cultures where the payment of large "gifts" is the norm follow local custom, library materials suppliers have learned what the norm is in doing business with libraries. Certain things such as free lunches and shuttle busses at conventions are acceptable in this environment, but bribery and price fixing are not. Librarians, by their behavior, can influence vendors to be more ethical, or less.

SUMMARY

To bring ethics to the fore:

1. Be conscious of ethics in relation to acquisitions.
2. Maintain high personal standards.
3. Encourage ethical behavior in others.
4. Broaden discussion of ethics and acquisitions within the profession.

This is not to say that librarians can control the ethics of this business, but that they can exert a positive or negative influence. Most vendors cite little awareness of unethical behavior on the part of librarians. More consciousness of this influence and more attention paid to ethical consideration might result in an even more positive situation. As one vendor put it, "most of us like to think of ourselves as ethical people in a dog-eat-dog world. You can be relatively ethical and do just as well. But if librarians start, in a big way, to deal unethically with us, we'll succumb."

It is worth thinking about. Maybe some librarians have been ethical out of naivete or lack of opportunity or because really big bucks just don't exist in this business, but it is to be hoped that librarians are and will be ethical through positive choice and that library materials vendors will behave in a like manner.

Ethical questions involving acquisitions librarians and materials vendors need to be probed. Instead of thinking that things are not bad, ethically speaking, the profession needs to open this Pandora's Box and see what comes out. Having given some thought to ethical questions in real situations and having explored the literature on the topic, we will each be better prepared for whatever ethical challenge is sure to confront us at some point in the future.

APPENDIX A

TRACKING LIBRARY MATERIALS PRICES

Prices will continue to be important both for their effect on library budgets and collections and as a continuing source of friction between libraries and their suppliers. Therefore, tracking pricing trends for various types of materials will remain necessary.

Ongoing data collection as described in Chapter 10 greatly simplifies assembling figures, understanding trends, and preparing reports.

The following sources of pricing and related economic information are readily available and affordable. Any given library will choose its preferred sources. Check-in records should be annotated so that the issues of serials containing current pricing information go directly to the person who maintains these data. In addition to these regularly published sources of pricing data, it is useful to be alert for articles on general economic trends, political activities, developments in the academic community, etc. that may affect libraries, wherever these articles may appear. Frequently, they are published in journals other than those directed toward the library profession. One's own general reading as well as clues from colleagues augmented by occasional literature searches all contribute to the development of a collection of useful information at one's fingertips. Of course, clippings and photocopies must be annotated with full citations.

LIBRARY, BOOK TRADE, AND GENERAL PUBLICATIONS

The Bookseller. London: J. Whitaker & Sons Ltd. Weekly.

> Statistics on British book output and prices, as well as articles on British publishing and bookselling.

The Bowker Annual. New York: R.R. Bowker.

> Includes data from *Publishers Weekly* with some useful additions, including data on British, German, and Latin American publications—all in one place; useful commentary, section on exchange rates, but always some months to over a year old.

Choice. Middletown, CT: Association of College and Research Libraries. Monthly except bimonthly in July/August.

The "College Book Price Index" appears in the March issue each year. Data are limited to books reviewed in *Choice* during the preceding year and show numbers of books published and average prices; includes retrospective data for comparative purposes.

Library Issues: Briefings for Faculty and Administrators. Ann Arbor: Mountainside Publishing. Bimonthly.

Up-to-date information on various developments in the library world; not limited to pricing issues.

Library Journal. New York: Bowker Magazine Group. Issued 21 times per year.

"Price Index for U.S. Periodicals" and "Price Index for U.S. Serial Services" are published in the April 15 issue each year. Tables and commentary track pricing trends for the preceding year with retrospective comparisons. Data are derived from the F.W. Faxon database. Other information relevant to pricing issues also appears occasionally.

Mann, Peter. *Average Prices of British Academic Books.* LISU British Academic Book Prices Report. Loughborough: Library and Information Statistics Unit, Loughborough University of Technology. Semiannual.

These figures are useful for tracking prices of British academic books; includes numbers of titles and average prices by subject categories as well as some retrospective data for comparison and commentary. Data are derived from the B.H. Blackwell database.

―――. *Average Prices of USA Academic Books.* LISU USA Academic Book Prices Report. Loughborough: Library and Information Statistics Unit, Loughborough University of Technology. Semi-annual.

Similar in format to the preceding, this publication tracks numbers of titles and average prices of academic books published in the U.S. Data are derived from the Blackwell North America database.

Newsletter on Serial Pricing Issues. Chapel Hill, NC: Edited and published by Marcia Tuttle.

Published for several years under the auspices of the American Library Association, now independent, this journal in electronic format is an essential first source for the most current information.

Publishers Weekly. Newton, MA: Cahners Pub. Co. Weekly, except for last week in Dec.; additional issues in Jan., Feb., and Aug.

"Book Price Averages and Output," preliminary figures published in March, final figures in the fall, for the preceding year for U.S. produced books in various categories (all hard and paperbacks; trade paperbacks; mass market; etc.).

The Wall Street Journal. New York: Dow Jones & Co. Daily except Sat., Sun. and legal holidays.

Daily exchange rate tables, articles on economic trends, developments in the publishing industry.

VENDOR INFORMATION

All major vendors track pricing trends. They produce pricing studies for publication and for distribution to clients. They also produce custom reports on materials supplied to customers on request. Some widely distribute studies of past pricing as well as predictions of future trends.

EBSCO's *Index Medicus*™, intended to be a serial publication, is a recent and innovative vendor study of pricing trends over time.

Custom reports may be broken down by material type, library fund, price, postage, service charge, etc. and show average prices for a given period of time.

Studies and predictions from various vendors can be studied and related to the library's own figures and purchasing patterns. If several vendors predict journal price increases within a very close range and the library has found its own figures to be in line with these vendors' figures in the past, more weight might be put on a certain percentage of expected increase than would otherwise be justified. These vendors have very sophisticated computer systems and can sometimes track a library's purchasing patterns and material specific costs more easily than can the library itself. If reports of this nature are received from vendors they should be used. Custom reports should be designed with care to ensure that they provide useful data.

By analyzing data from a number of sources in light of the local situation and keeping in mind the fact that any database can be flawed and skewed in various ways, librarians can distill much useful information.

APPENDIX B

KEEPING UP WITH VENDOR-RELATED ISSUES

What vendors are out there? What are they doing? What issues affect vendors and librarians?

There are a number of forums that bring vendors and librarians together as well as others where vendor-related issues may be discussed. Waiting for a sales representative to visit one's library is no way to keep up with vendors. Active participation with them and with other librarians in various settings will contribute much more to mutual understanding and respect. Some suggestions:

The Charleston Conference: Held each November in Charleston, SC, this is the primary occasion for librarians, vendors, and publishers to meet and to discuss issues. Papers presented at this conference are published, usually the following autumn.

American Library Association: Within ALA there are a number of opportunities for librarians and vendors to work on mutually important issues. Below are listed some of the primary ALA groups that deal with such issues. For a fuller understanding of ALA organizational structure and complete listing and description of all associations and subsidiary bodies, see the *Handbook of Organization* published annually by ALA.

1. Association for Library Collections and Technical Services (ALCTS)
   Publisher/Vendor Library Relations Committee
   AV Publisher/Distributor Library Relations Subcommittee
   Association of American Publishers - ALCTS Joint Committee
   Serials Pricing Issues Task Force
2. The Acquisition of Library Materials Section
   Acquisitions Committee
   Foreign Book Dealers Directories Series Subcommittee Guides Subcommittee
   Library Materials Price Index Committee
   Acquisition Librarians/Vendors of Library Materials Committee

155

3. The Serials Section
    Acquisitions Committee
    Committee to Study Serials Standards

Other ALCTS committee meeting and special programs are held in conjunction with ALA conferences and independently, many of which provide opportunities for confronting library/vendor issues. Service on such committees or attendance at their meetings provides valuable contact with vendors and exposure to vendor-related issues.

The National Acquisitions Conference: Held in a different location in the United States each year, this is a forum for the discussion of many kinds of issues relating to acquisitions including those related to vendor relations. Proceedings are independently published.

The North American Serials Interest Group (NASIG): A joint librarian/vendor group whose annual meeting each summer is a valuable forum for the discussion of serials and problems relating to them. Scholarships for attendance at the conference are offered to several library school students each year. Proceedings are published in *The Serials Librarian* the following winter.

Most conferences have vendor displays, the most noteworthy being the huge ALA annual meeting. Such occasions can be very useful and educational means of learning about vendors and talking with them about products, service, etc. Unfortunately the potential is sometimes diminished by the sheer number of people in the exhibit area, lack of time, and exhaustion.

Librarians can benefit from attending events not specifically designed for them such as The American Booksellers Association Convention. The Frankfurt Book Fair, other book fairs outside North America, antiquarian book fairs around the country, and the Denver Out-of-Print and Antiquarian Book Market Seminar all offer valuable experiences for librarians which can enhance their relationships with vendors.

For academic librarians with access to BITNET or Internet, ACQNET is a lively E-MAIL journal, edited by Christian Boissonnas at Cornell University. Anything and everything pertaining to acquisitions might appear here including issues relating to vendors.

The Newsletter on Serial Pricing Issues, described in Appendix A, is also a good means of keeping up with vendors as their activities relate to serial pricing.

Against the Grain (ATG), a journal published five times per year for attendees of the Charleston Conference, is a lively source of information about issues of importance to librarians and vendors, with contributions by both.

STANDARDS ORGANIZATIONS

Opportunities for participation in the development of information standards are open to librarians in North American through the following groups:

1. Book Industry Study Group, Inc., 160 Fifth Avenue, New York, NY 10010; parent organization of Book Industry Systems Advisory Committee (BISAC) and Serials Industry Systems Advisory Committee (SISAC), which develop draft standards that are eventually accepted and published as official United States standards by the National Information Standards Organization.
2. Canadian Telemark Agency, embracing the Canadian Book Industry Systems Advisory Committee, and the Canadian Serials Industry Systems Advisory Committee, which attempt to influence the development of U.S. and international standards so that they will accommodate Canadian requirements. Information about both groups is available from Lucy Bottomley, National Library of Canada, Ottawa.

INTERNSHIPS

Recently, there has been renewed interest in internships. Some librarians have arranged internships with vendors on their own. Nothing could be a more valuable aid to understanding the activities and viewpoint of vendors than working for one.

APPENDIX C

WHAT LIBRARIANS THINK OF VENDORS

Information about librarians' opinions regarding vendors has been collected in various ways: networking at conferences, published articles, comments in ACQNET, phone calls, and the results of a questionnaire mailed to 100 acquisitions librarians. Attempts to elicit complaints about vendors garnered very little comment. Response to the questionnaire was minimal. In no way a statistically significant survey, this collection of opinion does, however, provide some interesting insight into librarians' relationships with their materials suppliers. Overall, use of vendors and satisfaction with them was high and complaints few, while publishers as distributors received considerable criticism.

Perhaps one can conclude that lack of complaint is a good thing, that vendors are serving libraries well, and that librarians are generally satisfied. When there is cause for concern, such as with rising prices or with a publisher who decides to do its own distribution, librarians are seldom shy about expressing themselves. Nevertheless, complacency is dangerous and it is worthwhile to look closely at the comments of those who spoke.

The questionnaire asked for information about and satisfaction with North American and overseas book suppliers and subscription agents. Respondents were asked to characterize their libraries as academic, public, school, special, medical, or law. Responding libraries fell into each of those categories and ranged in size from 10,000 to two and a half million volumes. Number of vendors used ranged from one to 200, although such high numbers may have included publishers.

SELECTION OF VENDORS

Despite the wide diversity among the responding libraries, they were consistent in their high use of vendors. With the exception of law libraries that order much material directly from publishers, most libraries chose vendors for firm-ordered North American monographs 75 to 98 percent of the time. A few split orders more evenly between vendors and publishers or even favor direct orders. Foreign firm-ordered monographs were commonly ordered from vendors, sometimes to the exclusion of direct orders. Medical libraries varied from 100 percent from vendors to 100 percent direct. Similar high use of vendors for both North American and foreign periodicals subscriptions was apparent for all types of libraries, although a few mavericks may be as low as a 50-50 split between vendor-supplied subscriptions and direct orders. One public library orders all subscriptions direct. These responses correlated well with input on vendor use obtained otherwise.

Perhaps most interesting were answers to queries about why libraries use vendors in general and why they chose their particular suppliers. Many said that they use a vendor whenever possible. That is, if an item can be supplied by a vendor, it will be ordered from one. Items are ordered direct only as a last resort. Some will go direct on speciality items or for speed. One repeated as a sort of litany "faster, better, cheaper" as the rationale for using vendors. One person commented that ordering directly from publishers "is a hassle and consumes time I don't have." Service, discount, and speed of fulfillment were frequently mentioned as criteria for selecting vendors, and it appeared that librarians are aware of the relative strengths of various vendors and send orders to those vendors expected to service them best. Librarians also considered the seriousness of vendors, their past performance regarding claims, returns, service in general, and problem-solving ability. Also cited as incentives for using particular vendors were the availability of vendor-provided order forms, special prepayment programs, and management reports.

From foreign vendors, librarians also want billing in U.S. (or Canadian) dollars. One public library respondent commented that most vendors do not handle foreign titles, so they are ordered direct. Does this mean that this person is unaware of North American vendors' ability to supply certain foreign items, that they are unaware of vendors outside of North America, or that they truly order such unusual material that there are no vendors who would be able to supply it?

Librarians' choices of subscription agents are governed by much the same perceptions. Agents were generally used unless they could not supply or libraries were forbidden to use them. Several libraries mentioned ordering localized, obscure, or societal publications direct, echoing the widely held perception that agents do not handle such material well. However, one librarian stated that "anything worth spending my budget on is available through a vendor." Availability, price, and service were common themes.

In addition to ability to supply a wide variety of titles and general dependability, subscription agents are asked for prompt response to queries, "diligence in claiming," good billing practices, replacement of missing issues, and online services. There was a sense of urgency and somewhat higher expectations of subscription agents than for firm-order vendors.

PUBLISHERS

Another question asked librarians to describe problems encountered when ordering direct from publishers. This called forth some genuine ire on the part of the respondents. One said, "Everything: refusal to acknowledge returns, wrong and partial shipments, confusing the library account with others on campus, treating claims as orders, books and invoice sent separately and to different addresses, requiring prepayment, non-receipt of materials (sometimes prepaid), refusal to go through vendors," delays, lack of responsiveness, lack of personal contact, difficulties in communication, lack of availability of material, billing problems, nuisance paperwork that wastes staff time, delays, and lack of discount. Librarians complained that it is sometimes difficult to identify a company's correct address and that orders sent to one company may be billed by another. This causes great havoc in online systems in particular.

SERVICES

Services that librarians would like to see vendors offer include online order, reporting, invoicing, and electronic mail services, more electronic ways to facilitate claiming, ways to check other libraries' serial check-in records, and electronic interfaces with all major vendors. Nothing was mentioned more often than these kinds of online connections with vendors. Those that are available now are appreciated, but librarians want more such services and from more vendors. MARC tapes from *all* vendors are desirable as well. Some of the "wants" noted here *are* available from certain vendors, but apparently not from those used by the librarians who want them. One noted always being interested in new electronic interfaces with vendors.

In order for such online services to be offered broadly to the library community, materials vendors, librarians, and library systems vendors must work together to ensure that technical standards are adopted that will make such linkages practical. Some materials vendors have adapted to the requirements of certain major online library systems or have offered their own systems, but such an approach is too costly and too limited to continue. Standards are the foundation that must be built first so that systems will be able to communicate readily with each other.

Wants other than electronic hookups were mentioned as well: "a better discount is the main thing," said one respondent. Some appreciate vendors' abilities to inform them of new publications and want such services to continue. A "menu" of services from which to pick and choose was mentioned. A special library wants more creativity in designing approval plans while another wants notification of certain subject area materials' availability, but not an approval plan. At the no frills end of the spectrum was the respondent who wants the vendors to "just supply what I need."

Opinion on how services should be paid for was almost evenly split between those who feel service should be included as part of the overall cost of materials and those who wanted a "supermarket" approach. The "no frills" voice was heard here as well from one who wrote: "We pay for the books, etc. What else *should* we pay for?"

BEYOND THE LOWER 48

Effort was made to solicit comment from libraries beyond the contiguous 48 states. Canadian libraries and libraries in Puerto Rico and some Pacific Islands responded. The response rate was actually higher from some of these locations than from those in the mainland United States. Because of their "out-of-the-mainstream" situations, these librarians' comments merit special attention.

Canadian respondents choose vendors for the same reasons others do and have much the same expectations and complaints. However, they have additional comments relative to their own particular situations. In fact, one mentioned that there were a number of complaints that were probably particular to Canadian libraries, but did not enumerate them. Some specific complaints included publishers and vendors who advertise toll-free telephone numbers that cannot be used by Canadians and postage-paid envelopes with U.S. postage only. Also mentioned was the lack of Canadian rights for U.S. publishers resulting in books being unobtainable in Canada. According to one respondent, the Canadian Goods and Services Tax apparently has caused "many U.S. publishers to refuse to do business with Canadian libraries." There are enough hints of trouble here to make one wonder if more attention should be paid to the Canadian market by both vendors and publishers. Some, if not all, major materials vendors have complied with the requirements of the G.S.T. If publishers have not, this may be an area where vendors have an added service to offer Canadian libraries. Of course if publishers who refuse to deal with vendors also refuse to sell direct to Canadian libraries, there is little to be done, but it is hard to believe that they would completely write off an entire market in this way.

The Puerto Rican respondent noted no special circumstances or complaints despite using a mixture of vendors and publishers for firm-ordered monographs and ordering all periodicals direct. She did note that sometimes vendors "do not fulfill our terms."

Two librarians from the Pacific responded, both having quite different ordering patterns. One uses vendors for 90 percent of firm-orders and 99.9 percent of periodicals. The other obtains only a third of firm-ordered monographs and 70 percent of periodicals from vendors. Both indicated moderate satisfaction with their vendors. They use the common criteria of price, service, and availability of desired materials. A certain publisher came under fire once again. One noted that vendor errors have greater effect when distance makes resolution a very long-term affair, such as when the wrong book is shipped. Nevertheless, a major North American book vendor was mentioned as providing some desired services such as a prepayment program and good discounts.

COMPLAINTS ABOUT VENDORS

Lest the high levels of satisfaction and the negative comments about ordering direct from publishers cause vendors to gloat, the respondents also had complaints about vendors themselves. It seems that librarians' expectations of vendors are very high, perhaps unrealistically so, and while they claimed to be somewhat satisfied or very satisfied most often, they also knew where their vendors were falling short. One librarian stated that they are not shy about changing vendors and do so unless they *are* very satisfied. These were open-ended questions in which respondents were encouraged to say whatever they wished about library materials suppliers. Vendors' names were not requested, but some were mentioned in both praise and complaint nevertheless.

Vendors were faulted for slow or non-shipment, errors in shipping, incomplete shipments, duplicate shipments, sloppy record keeping, being slower than local bookstores to provide current popular titles, discounts not matching contract, incomprehensible discount schedule, failure to supply status reports. A book supplier was heartily criticized for rejecting orders with the notice "cannot find ISBN" even when the library supplied this number. It does seem that a competent book dealer should be able to locate a book even without an ISBN!

One person found a vendor's customer service office unresponsive and stated that "fifteen years as a customer should count for something." There was also the impression that small libraries are discriminated against.

Subscription agents were taken to task for sloppy claims procedures. Claiming and its frequent lack of success is a common complaint anywhere serials people gather. Agents who reply that it is too late to claim because the publisher requires claims within a specified period infuriate librarians who did claim within that period. Complaints also focused on increasing numbers of claims and paying twice for a missed item. "Serials agents need to work harder with publishers and libraries on this," said one respondent. Added charges were criticized for making "sensible budgeting nearly impossible." Another cited the "increasing 'don't give a damn' attitude of major serials agents."

On the other hand, certain subject-oriented suppliers of both books and periodicals received high praise from special libraries, sometimes in pointed contrast to large generalized suppliers.

IMPLICATIONS

There are some implications in all this for acquisitions librarians and vendors, both of whom may see themselves in the comments recorded here, as well as implications for their partnership. Those who responded to the questionnaire expressed sentiments largely reflected in the current literature and in the content of recent conferences.

The comments recorded here, especially when considered in light of vendors' viewpoints mentioned throughout the preceding chapters, lead one to the following conclusions:

- There is indeed a partnership between librarians and vendors.
- For the most part, both parties are genuinely interested in making the partnership work.
- That partnership often needs more attention from both parties.
- Vendors fill a much needed niche as middleman between publisher and library. Perhaps librarian and vendor can join forces to make this clearer to publishers.
- Technical standards to facilitate data interchange cannot come too soon; both librarians and vendors need to work hard at achieving them.
- A varied marketplace will continue to serve the library world best with its diversity of needs from small to large, general to specialized, no frills to multiple service.
- Communication is critical. Do the vendors these librarians complained about know how these customers feel? One would hope that they would care enough to do something about it if they knew. Have the vendors adequately explained their capabilities and points of view?

- Subscription agents, particularly, might pay more attention to claiming and overall service.
- Quality service *is* recognized. It is nearly impossible to "be all things to all people." Those vendors who received the most enthusiastic praise have carved a niche for themselves and provide superior service to it.

BIBLIOGRAPHY

Bibliographical references are arranged by chapter for ease in linking them to the subject matter covered. These references are not intended to be exhaustive. They are highly selective, even idiosyncratic, listing only those sources found most pertinent to the subjects under discussion. Wherever possible, published bibliographies have been included that will provide a greater range of references. It is hoped that these chapter bibliographies will lead the reader into a subject rather than to provide the final answer on any topic. Given the rapid rate of change in acquisitions today, they are of course not perfectly current. Each is followed by a brief annotation indicating its usefulness.

CHAPTER 1: SOME BASICS

BOOKS

Melcher, Daniel, and Margaret Saul. *Melcher on Acquisition.* Chicago: American Library Association, 1971.

> If one reads only a single book on acquisitions work, this is it; practical, sensible, and forthright.

ARTICLES

Barker, Joseph W. "Acquisitions and Collection Development: 2001." *Library Acquisitions: Practice & Theory* 12 (2): 243-248 (1988).

> The clearest view of what lies ahead for a large research library's acquisitions operation, with implications for libraries of other types as well.

Boissonnas, Christian M. "Desperately Seeking Status: Acquisitions Librarians in Academic Libraries." *Library Acquisitions: Practice & Theory* 15 (3): 349-354 (1991).

> Acquisitions librarians have an essential role to play for which they should be properly trained and which they must be willing to assume.

Hewitt, Joe. "On the nature of acquisitions." *Library Resources & Technical Services* 33 (2): 105-122 (1989).

> Essential reading for all acquisitions librarians and their staffs, this article explains unequivocally the complexity, importance, and unique nature of acquisitions work.

Schmidt, Karen A. "The Education of the Acquisitions Librarian: A Survey of ARL Acquisitions Librarians." *Library Resources & Technical Services* 35 (1): 7-22 (1991).

Schmidt's study indicates that inclusion of acquisitions in library school curricula would benefit the profession as a whole.

CHAPTER 2: WHAT LIES AHEAD?

THE ELECTRONIC FUTURE

Hawks, Carol Pitts. "Automated Library Systems: What Next?" *Serials Librarian* 21 (2/3): 87-96 (1991).

> A cogent and exciting view of the future of library automation especially as it relates to acquisitions and serials.

Intner, Sheila S. "A New Paradigm for Access to Serials." *The Serials Librarian* 19 (3/4): 131-161 (1991).

> A plea for providing fuller bibliographic access to the contents of serials through electronic access to more in-depth cataloging and full texts of publications.

Weber, Robert. "Libraries Without Walls?" *Publishers Weekly* 237:S20-S22 (June 8, 1990).

> An overview of the current state and future prospects of the truly electronic library with unlimited access to distant information.

Young, Peter. "Evolving Knowledge Resource Access Systems." In *Collection Development: Survival Tactics in an Age of Less,* 1-14. New York: The Library Association of the City University of New York, 1992.

> Presented as the keynote address at the 1991 City University of New York Library Association Collection Development Institute, "Survival Tactics in an Age of Less," this paper eloquently and with originality examines the current state and possible future directions of academic library information supply.

STANDARDS—ARTICLES

"American National Standards for Libraries, Publishers, and Information Services." In *The Bowker Annual* (1990/91), 556-563, New York: R. R. Bowker.

> The current status of National Information Standards Organization (NISO) standards; appears annually.

Lane, Liz. "Library Technical Standards and the Online Environment: A Current Bibliography." *Library High Tech Bibliography* 8:131-135 (1990).

A useful source for materials published 1984-1989; includes bibliographies listing earlier materials; annotated.

Mutter, John. "Parlez-Vous X12? Do You Speak EDI?" *Publishers Weekly* 237:27-30 (Nov. 9, 1990).

For those who have never heard of X-12, this explains, in layman's terms, what it is, what it can do, and how it is being applied in the book trade.

Schwartz, Frederick E. "The EDI Horizon: Implementing an ANSI X12 Pilot Project at the Faxon Company." *The Serials Librarian* 19 (3/4): 39-57 (1991).

This paper clearly explains the potential that EDI offers libraries and their vendors and what needs to be done to realize this potential.

Swain, Leigh. "Message Handling Systems and Electronic Data Interchange: An Introduction to Converging Standards for Electronic Messaging." *IFLA Journal* 16:204-214 (1990).

Although somewhat technical, this article is essential for understanding the basics, current status, and future prospects of OSI.

STANDARDS—PERIODICALS

Information Standards Quarterly. Gaithersburg, Md.: National Information Standards Organization. Vol. 1, no. 1 (Jan. 1989)- . Quarterly.

Essential for keeping abreast of developments in information standards in the U.S.

Journal of Interlibrary Loan & Information Supply. Binghamton, N.Y.: Haworth Press. Vol. 1, no. 1 (1990)- .

Frequent articles on technical standards relating to resource sharing issues and regular column "The World of OSI" by Leigh Swain are indispensable.

FULL TEXT DOCUMENT DELIVERY

Boyne, Walter J., and Hernan Otano. "Direct Document Capture and Full Text Indexing: An Introduction to the National Air and Space Museum System." *Library Hi Tech* 8:7-14 (1984).

A description of an innovative system developed at the NASM.

Dale, Larry. "Document Scanning: a New Technology for Library Use." *Technicalities* 9 (1): 4-6 (Jan. 1989).

An introduction to optical scanning of texts for conversion to computer files both for internal use and as a patron service.

Detemple, Wendelin. "Future enhancements for full text databases." *Online Review* 13:155-160 (April 1989).

As full text databases become more widespread, they will become easier to use and offer continued enhancements.

Korwitz, Ulrich. "ADONIS: Between Myth and Reality: Trial Document Supply Using CD-ROM Technology." *IFLA Journal* 16 (2) :215-219 (1990).

A description of a project providing CD-ROM access to all articles from 224 biomedical journals published in 1987 and 1988 from a European viewpoint. Expresses enthusiasm for the concept, despite imperfections.

Meiseles, Linda. "The ADONIS Project: The Brooklyn Experience." *Advances in Library Resources Sharing* 1:166-175 (1990).

ADONIS as experienced by an American library; descriptive rather than evaluative.

Parkhurst, Carol A., ed. *Library Perspectives on NREN.* Chicago: Library and Information Technology Association, a Division of the American Library Association, 1990.

A thorough look at NREN, what it is, how it has developed, how various types of libraries can make use of it and similar networks, what the future may bring. Essential reading.

Rice, Patricia Ohl. "From Acquisitions to Access." *Library Acquisitions: Practice & Theory* 14 (1): 15-21 (1990).

Discusses the academic library of the future as a disseminator of scholarly articles in electronic format.

CHAPTER 3: CHOOSING BOOK VENDORS

ARTICLES

Carter, Robert A. "Taking Aim at the Library Market." *Publishers Weekly* 237:S6-S16 (June 8, 1990).

Publishers' view of the library market.

Clark, Mae M. "RTSD/RS Library/Vendor Relations Discussion Group." *Library Acquisitions: Practice & Theory* 12 (2): 437-438 (1988).

A brief discussion, from the 1987 Charleston Conference, of cost-plus (net) pricing and modular pricing.

Fast, Barry, and Corrie Marsh. "Issues in Library-Vendor Relations." *Against the Grain* 2 (2): 14-15, 35 (April 1990).

> Flat discounts are compared with variable discounts and the librarian's role in negotiating discounts is discussed.

Leonhardt, Thomas W. "Buying Direct vs. Third Party Buying." *Library Acquisitions: Practice & Theory* 12 (2): 259-260 (1988).

> Briefly discusses the usefulness of library materials vendors and the relative strengths of small and large vendors.

Marsh, Corrie V. "Net Book Pricing." *Library Acquisitions: Practice & Theory* 12 (2): 169-176 (1988).

> Results of a study aimed at identifying net prices and determining the accuracy of billing.

Quinn, Judy. "The 'Selling' of the Book in the 1990s." *Library Journal* 115:142-147 (Feb. 15, 1990).

> A discussion among publishers, vendors, and librarians about marketing books to libraries, what libraries want, and how best to provide it.

BOOKS

Eaglen, Audrey. *Buying Books: A How-To-Do-It Manual for Librarians.* New York, London: Neal-Schuman Publishers, Inc., 1989.

> This current book is a comprehensive guide to purchasing in print domestic firm-ordered monographs directly from publishers and from vendors. Included is a selected list of U.S. book vendors.

VENDOR IDENTIFICATION GUIDES

"Acquisitions From the Third World: A Special Issue of Library Acquisitions: Practice & Theory." *Library Acquisitions: Practice & Theory* 6(2) (1982).

> An old, but thorough and valuable guide to obtaining this significant but often difficult to acquire material.

The African Book World & Press: A Directory. 4th ed. London: Zell, 1989.

> Updated every few years, this comprehensive guide provides information on publishers, booksellers, libraries, book industry and library associations, and major printers as well as a list of periodicals and newspapers throughout Africa.

American Book Trade Directory. New York: R.R. Bowker. Annual

Lists retailers and wholesalers of books and wholesalers of magazines in the United States and Canada; includes antiquarian booksellers and dealers in foreign language books.

Block, David, and Howard L. Karno. *A Directory of Vendors of Latin American Library Materials.* 3rd ed., rev. and enl. Bibliography and Reference Series, 22. Madison, Wis.: Seminar on the Acquisition of Latin American Library Materials, Secretariat, Memorial Library, University of Wisconsin-Madison, 1988.

Not perfectly current, but essential; most useful if annotated to reflect local experiences.

Downey, J.A. "The Acquisition of Social Science Literature from the Anglophone Caribbean: A British Perspective." *Library Acquisitions: Practice & Theory* 9 (2): 121-145 (1985).

Discusses why and how to collect English language books from the Caribbean with extensive bibliographical notes and a list of vendors.

International Literary Market Place: The Directory of the International Book Publishing Industry. New York: R.R. Bowker. Annual.

Essential guide to publishing and bookselling worldwide; includes directories of remainder dealers and booksellers by country.

Literary Market Place: The Directory of the American Book Publishing Industry with Industry Yellow Pages. New York: R.R. Bowker. Annual.

The basic guide to book publishing and distribution in North America; includes directories of remainder dealers and booksellers, including lists by area of activity (approval plans, schools, general trade, maps and atlases, etc.)

North Carolina Center for Independent Higher Education, Library Purchasing Committee. *Directory of Foreign Monograph Vendors Serving Libraries in North Carolina.* Raleigh, N.C.: 1990.

Detailed entries for 147 vendors in the U.S. and abroad supplying foreign monographs; indexed by country and language of publication. A useful addition to any acquisitions department reference shelf.

Publishers, distributors and wholesalers of the United States. New York: R. R. Bowker, 1990.

This massive compilation provides access by name, geographic and type of activity indexes, toll-free numbers, and publisher discount information; frequently updated.

Tao, Hanyu. "How to Acquire Chinese Materials from the People's Republic of China: An Easy Way to Solve the Mystery." *Library Acquisitions: Practice & Theory* 13 (1): 11-31 (1989).

> A very useful, practical guide to purchasing materials published in the People's Republic of China; includes lists of North American sources as well as those in the PRC and Hong Kong.

Who Distributes What & Where. New York: R.R. Bowker. Annual

> Publishers and distributors worldwide are listed with name and geographic indexes.

CHAPTER 4: CHOOSING SERIALS VENDORS

ARTICLES

Barker, Joseph W. "Unbundling Serials Vendors' Service Charges: Are We Ready?" *Serials Review* 16 (2): 33-43 (Summer 1990).

> A lucid explanation of the promises and risks involved in separately pricing certain services commonly absorbed by an amorphous service charge.

Kuntz, Harry. "Serials Agents: Selection and Evaluation." *The Serials Librarian* 2 (2): 139-150 (Winter 1977).

> Basic guidelines for selecting subscription agents.

Merriman, J.B. "The Work of a Periodicals Agent." *The Serials Librarian* 14 (3/4): 17-36 (1988).

> A thorough explanation of the role of a subscription agent as seen by the director of B.H. Blackwell's Periodicals Division.

Prichard, R.J. "Serials Acquisitions: The Relation Between Serials Librarian and Subscription Agent." *The Serials Librarian* 14 (3/4): 5-10 (1988).

> The strengths and weaknesses of subscription agents and direct ordering are explored by a British librarian.

Schmidt, Karen A. "Choosing a Serials Vendor." *The Serials Librarian* 15 (3/4): 11-16 (1988)

> Basic advice on selecting a supplier of serials.

BOOKS

Basch, N. Bernard, and Judy McQueen. *Buying Serials: A How-To-Do-It Manual for Librarians.* New York: Neal-Schuman, 1990.

Basch, whose experience is with American subscription agents, is an unabashed proponent of unbundling serials costs and urges librarians to negotiate for lower service charges.

Katz, Bill, and Peter Gellatly. *Guide to Magazine and Serial Agents.* New York: R.R. Bowker, 1975.

Despite its age, this book is still useful, especially for the novice. Information should be verified through direct contact with suppliers.

Perryman, Wayne R., and Lenore Wilkes, comps. *International Subscription Agents; an Annotated Directory.* 5th ed. Chicago: American Library Association, 1986.

This essential guide to subscription agents includes North American agents as well as others throughout the world. It is currently under revision with a new edition expected in the early 1990s.

Singleton, Alan. *The Role of Subscription Agents with a Supplementary Report on UK Libraries' Trade with Agents* by Alan Cooper. BL (R&D) report, no. 5621. Leicester: Primary Communications Research Center, University of Leicester, 1981.

This is a succinct explanation of what subscription agents do; useful despite its age.

CHAPTER 5: BECOMING PARTNERS

ARTICLES

Abel, Richard. "Players in the Knowledge Transfer Enterprise." *Library Acquisitions: Practice & Theory* 12 (2): 159-161 (1988).

A major figure in library bookselling urges an alliance between libraries and their suppliers in order to facilitate the flow of information.

Berry, John. "The Enlightened Vendor." *Library Journal* 113:4 (July 1988).

Editorial comment urging greater cooperation and trust, and a less adversarial approach, between vendors and libraries.

Burroughs, Robert. "Full Speed Ahead: Book Wholesaling in the 1990s." *Library Journal* 115:157-159 (Feb. 15, 1990).

Expectations and attitudes among suppliers (including publishers) and librarians that may enhance book supply in the coming decade aided by technological developments.

Jasper, Richard P. "Academic Libraries and Firm Order Vendors: What They Want of Each Other." *The Acquisitions Librarian* 3:83-95 (1991).

A revealing look at the sometimes unrealistic expectations vendors and librarians have of each other.

Maddox, Jane. "The Serials Acquisition Partnership." *The Serials Librarian* 17 (3/4): 87-92 (1990).

Maddox, an American librarian who represents a European vendor, spells out the values and risks of the vendor/librarian partnership and urges that the librarian be knowledgeable.

Merriman, John B. "Publisher, Vendor, Librarian—Uneasy Alliance." *Library Acquisitions: Practice & Theory* 12 (2): 155-158 (1988).

Good perspective on the roles of and problems faced by these three players in the information game.

Secor, John R. "Scholarly Bookselling: An Evolution in Progress." *Library Acquisitions: Practice & Theory* 12:187-190 (1988).

The president of Yankee Book Peddler spells out his view of the relationship between publishers, vendors, and librarians.

Sexton, Mark. "The New Look in Library Distribution." *Publishers Weekly* 237 (23): S17-S19 (June 8, 1990).

Improved communication and technological enhancements help vendors respond to library demands.

Shirk, Gary M. "The Wondrous Web: Reflections of Library Acquisitions and Vendor Relationships." *The Acquisitions Librarian.* 5:1-20 (1991).

A librarian, currently vice president of Yankee Book Peddler, urges libraries to make a strong commitment to a vendor, forming a "strategic alliance."

Somers, Sally. "Vendor/Library Relations: A Perspective." *Library Acquisitions: Practice & Theory* 11 (2): 135-138 (1987).

A librarian's view of and warning to vendors who seek the library's business.

Tuttle, Marcia. "The Serials Manager's Obligation." *Library Resources & Technical Services* 31 (2): 135-147 (1987).

Essential reading for any librarian involved in obtaining serials.

BOOKS

Katz, Bill, ed. *Vendors and Library Acquisitions.* New York: Haworth Press, 1991.

Articles by vendors and librarians discuss various issues relating to monograph and serial acquisitions and approval plans. Also published as *The Acquisitions Librarian*, no. 5

CHAPTER 6: CONTRACTS AND BIDDING

ARTICLES

Boyer, Calvin J. "State-Wide Contracts for Library Materials: An Analysis of the Attendant Dysfunctional Consequences." *College and Research Libraries* 35 (2): 86-94 (March 1974).

> Boyer clearly sets forth the negative consequences for states, libraries, and vendors of statewide library materials contracts.

BOOKS

Melcher, Daniel, and Margaret Saul. "The Fallacy of the Bid Process." In *Melcher on Acquisition*, 46-55. Chicago: American Library Association, 1971.

> Shows in no uncertain terms why bidding does not work well for books.

Together, Boyer and Melcher provide ample evidence for why libraries should be left to purchase materials on their own, free of government-imposed bidding procedures.

CHAPTER 7: APPROVAL PLANS

ARTICLES

Barker, Joseph W. "Vendor Studies Redux: Evaluating the Approval Plan Option From Within." *Library Acquisitions: Practice & Theory* 13 (2): 133-141 (1989).

> This analysis of domestic and foreign approval plans at Berkeley indicates that they do not save staff time and that domestic plans more successfully provided essential core materials than did European plans.

Kruger, Betsy. "U.K. Books and Their U.S. Imprints: A Cost and Duplication Study." *Library Acquisitions: Practice & Theory* 15 (3): 301-312 (1991).

> Kruger's data indicate that most British books desired by the University of Illinois at Urbana-Champaign are published in the U.S. within 12 months of their appearance in Britain.

Nardini, Robert F. "How is the Approval Plan Doing?" In *Conference on Acquisitions, Budgets, and Collections. Proceedings*, compiled and edited by David C. Genaway, 345-358. Canfield, Ohio: Genaway & Associates Inc., 1990.

Historical review of approval plans, concluding that they are "here to stay"; extensive bibliography.

Reidelbach, John H., and Gary M. Shirk. "Selecting an Approval Plan Vendor: A Step-By-Step Process." *Library Acquisitions: Practice & Theory* 7 (2): 115-122 (1983).

This and the following two articles by the same authors are essential reading for libraries selecting approval plan vendors. This article sets forth a ten-step process for selecting a vendor once the decision has been made to implement a plan or move an existing plan to a new vendor.

———. "Selecting an Approval Plan Vendor II: Comparative Vendor Data." *Library Acquisitions: Practice & Theory* 8 (3): 157-202 (1984).

Eight major U.S. approval plan vendors are compared. Now unfortunately out-of-date, but still a useful guide for libraries wishing to conduct similar comparisons.

———. "Selecting an Approval Plan Vendor III: Academic Librarians' Evaluations of Eight United States Approval Plan Vendors." *Library Acquisitions: Practice & Theory* 9 (3): 177-260 (1985).

The experiences of over 100 academic libraries with domestic approval plans with eight named vendors are discussed. Also dated but valuable for insights it provides into what libraries want from approval plan vendors and how well these needs were met.

Rossi, Gary J. "Library Approval Plans: A Selected, Annotated Bibliography." *Library Acquisitions: Practice & Theory* 11 (1): 3-34 (1987).

A very inclusive bibliography of descriptive and evaluative material on approval plans, listed chronologically from 1957 to 1986.

St. Clair, Gloriana, and Jane Treadwell. "Science and Technology Approval Plans Compared." *Library Resources & Technical Services* 33 (4): 382-392 (1989).

One of the best analytical studies of library materials supply, this article clearly shows that the vendor a library uses for a sci-tech approval plan definitely affects the materials the plan will supply.

Warzala, Martin. "Acquisition of Monographic Series: Approval Plan Versus Standing Order." *Library Acquisitions: Practice & Theory* 15 (3): 313-327 (1991).

This paper presents the thesis that under certain circumstances it may be more economical to purchase monographs in series through approval plans rather than on standing order.

Wilden-Hart, Marion. "The Long-Term Effects of Approval Plans." *Library Resources & Technical Services* 14(3): 400-406 (1970).

A thoughtful and far-sighted article that should be read by all involved with approval plans.

BOOKS

Association of Research Libraries, Office of Management Studies. *Approval Plans.* (SPEC Kit, no. 141) Washington D.C.: 1988.

Valuable for libraries considering approval plans, this kit contains the results of a survey of 94 ARL libraries regarding their use of approval plans plus information on evaluating vendors, profiles, examples of forms, etc. and bibliography.

Cargill, Jennifer S., and Brian Alley. *Practical Approval Plan Management.* Phoenix, Ariz.: Oryx Press, 1979.

This is a useful nuts-and-bolts guide to selecting and maintaining an approval plan, although evaluation is not emphasized and detailed information from a few specific vendors is not current; slights other competent approval plan vendors.

CHAPTER 8: OUT OF THE MAIN STREAM

DIRECTORIES

AV Market Place: The Complete Business Directory of: Audio, Audio Visual, Computer Systems, Film, Video, Programming with Industry Yellow Pages. New York: R.R. Bowker.

Numerous indexes provide comprehensive access to audio-video products, their makers and suppliers, as well as support services in the U.S. and Canada. Essential for any library buying A-V materials.

CD-ROMS in Print: An International Guide. Westport, Conn.: Meckler. Annual.

A comprehensive guide to CD-ROMs in print with all pertinent data needed to order, including distributors for each item; available in print or CD-ROM formats.

Directory of Electronic Publications, 2d ed. Washington, D.C.: Association of Research Libraries, 1992.

This comprehensive directory includes journals, newsletters, and scholarly discussion groups. Each item is fully described with information on how to subscribe, send submissions, and how to access. Available online and in print form and updated regularly.

Microsoft CD-ROM Yearbook. Redmond, Wash.: Microsoft Press. Annual.

This comprehensive yet compact resource brings together current articles mostly reprinted from a variety of journals as well as CD-ROM title list with descriptions and specifications, and lists of data preparation houses, disc drives, retrieval systems and mastering and replication facilities. Essential for understanding this rapidly developing field.

Veaner, A., and A. Meckler, eds. *Microform Market Place*. Weston, Conn.: Microform Review Inc.

The basic directory of microform publishers, commercial and non-commercial, worldwide; published every two years.

Worldwide Government Directory, With International Organizations. Bethesda, Md.: Cambridge Information Group Directories, Inc. Published every other year.

Lists government agencies, including United Nations and other quasi-governmental international bodies, giving name, address, telephone, telex, forms of address. No descriptive material or list of publications but useful for contacting government agencies around the world.

ARTICLES

Cady, Susan A. "The Electronic Revolution in Libraries: Microfilm Déjà Vu?" *College & Research Libraries* 51:374-386 (July 1990).

The author explores the possibility that electronic formats will fall short of their initial promise, much as microforms have.

Johnson, Peggy. "CD-ROM: Issues in Acquisition." *Technicalities* 9 (3): 6-8 (March 1989).

A straightforward discussion of issues such as standards, costs, and license agreements relating to CD-ROM purchase.

Sabosik, Patricia E. "Electronic Subscriptions." *The Serials Librarian* 19 (3/4): 59-70 (1991).

The author places the current status of electronic subscriptions in a historical context, discusses current issues, and suggests future directions in the development of the electronic library.

Shill, Harold B. and Sandra K. Peterson. "Is Government Information in Your Library's Future? The Politics of Electronic Dissemination, 1989." *College & Research Libraries News* 8:649-659 (1989).

The authors discuss the impact of the shift to electronic formats and commercial distribution of U.S. federal government information and warn that current trends, if continued, may limit access to that information.

CHAPTER 9: OUT-OF-PRINT

ARTICLES

Barker, Joseph W., and others. "Organizing Out-of-Print and Replacement Acquisitions for Effectiveness, Efficiency, and the Future." *Library Acquisitions: Practice & Theory* 14 (2): 137-163 (1990).

An excellent argument for a well-organized, policy-based, centralized operation to handle all aspects of acquiring out-of-print materials.

Kim, Ung Chon. "A Comparison of Two Out-of-Print Book Buying Methods." *College & Research Libraries* 34 (5): 258-264 (1973).

Kim concludes that advertising for desired out-of-print material is more cost effective than searching dealers' catalogs.

Miletich, Ivo. "Medium Size University Library Acquisitions Department and Use of Second-Hand Book Suppliers." In *Conference on Acquisitions, Budgets, and Collections. Proceedings*, compiled and edited by David C. Genaway, 333-344. Canfield, Ohio: Genaway & Associates, 1990.

Practical tips from a librarian who takes the out-of-print market seriously.

Nuzzo, David J. "A Reasonable Approach to Out-of-Print Procurement Using dBase II or dBase III." *Library Acquisitions: Practice & Theory* 11 (2): 165-180 (1987).

Using a PC to match the library's want list with dealers' catalogs permits efficient pursuit of out-of-print items not located through advertisements.

ADVICE AND PHILOSOPHY

Cather, James Pat. "Librarians and Booksellers: Forming a Durable Bond." *AB Bookman's Weekly* 85:2624-2632 (June 18, 1990).

A bookseller offers advice to librarians on how to form a workable relationship.

Gordon, Vesta Lee. "Buying O.P. Books: A Guide for Librarians." *AB Bookman's Weekly* 85:2633-2637 (June 18, 1990).

Practical information from a former librarian, now a book dealer, to aid librarians in making use of the out-of-print book trade.

Garnet, Anthony. "A Worm's-Eye View of the Out-of-Print Market." In *Conference on Acquisitions, Budgets, and Collections. Proceedings*, compiled and edited by David C. Genaway, 179-187. Canfield, Ohio: Genaway & Associates, 1990.

Another dealer offers his insights into how librarians can best make use of out-of-print dealers.

Landesman, Margaret. "Selling Out-of-Print Books to Libraries." *AB Bookman's Weekly* 74:3184-3192 (November 5, 1984).

Advice from an acquisitions librarian for booksellers wishing to sell out-of-print material to libraries.

Marsh, Corrie. "There Really Is a Different Book Market Out There: Reflections on the 10th Annual Out-of-Print & Antiquarian Book Market Seminar, University of Denver, August 7-12, 1988." *Library Acquisitions: Practice & Theory* 12:445-448 (1988).

Reflections on the seminar, all too rarely frequented by librarians, at which booksellers share experiences and offer advice.

Schenck, William Z. "The Acquisition of Out-of-Print Books." *AB Bookman's Weekly* 68:4015-4032 (Dec. 7, 1981).

A librarian explores various means of obtaining out-of-print material.

FINDING DEALERS

AB Bookman's Weekly. New York: AB Bookman Publications, 1948-.

This periodical is essential reading for its articles, ads, listings of book fairs, etc.

American Book Collector. *Directory of Specialized American Bookdealers*. New York: The Moretus Press, Inc..

Several thousand North American dealers are listed in geographical, subject, and alphabetical sections in this serial publication.

The Library Bookseller: Books Wanted by College and University Libraries. West Orange, N.J.: Albert Saifer. Biweekly.

The place to advertise for needed out-of-print books.

"Wholesale Remainder Dealers." In *Literary Market Place: The Directory of the American Book Publishing Industry with Industry Yellow Pages*. New York: R.R. Bowker. Annual.

Easily overlooked, this section of *Literary Market Place* is invaluable to those wishing to pursue the almost out-of-print market.

Robinson, Ruth E., and Daryush Farudi, comps. *Buy Books Where Sell Books Where: A Directory of Out of Print Booksellers and their Author-subject Specialities*, 1990-1991. Morgantown, W.Va.: Ruth E. Robinson, Books, 1990.

Geographical and subject indexes to U.S. book dealers; frequent new editions.

CHAPTER 10: THE PRICING PROBLEM

ARTICLES

See Appendix A for further suggestions on keeping abreast of pricing issues.

Association of Research Libraries. *Report of the ARL Serials Prices Project.* Washington, D.C. (1989).

This is the much discussed "ARL Report." Some publishers objected to its criticism of certain publisher practices.

Association of Research Libraries. "Serials Control and Deselection Project." System and Procedures Exchange Center. SPEC Kit, no. 147. Washington, D.C.: Office of Management Studies, 1988.

This kit contains an assemblage of documents from ARL libraries relating to documenting and dealing with budget shortfalls due to escalating serials prices.

Cox, Meg. "Book Publishers Face a Painful Austerity After Lavish Spending." *The Wall Street Journal*, Nov. 21, 1989: A1;6.

Difficulties faced by publishers due to their own practices may lead to higher prices and reduced wholesale discounts.

Dougherty, Richard M., and Brenda L. Johnson. "Periodical Price Escalation: A Library Response." *Library Journal* 113:27-29 (May 15, 1988).

A warning to publishers that libraries cannot absorb continued high book and journal prices and will find alternatives.

Fortney, Lynn M., and Victor A. Basile. *Index Medicus™ Price Study: 1986-1990.* 1st ed. Birmingham, Ala. EBSCO Subscription Services, Biomedical Division, 1990.

Revealing data show by subject and country how prices for certain journals have fluctuated during the years studied. The authors expect to repeat this study annually.

Hamaker, Charles A., and Stuart Grinell. "Cost Analysis of Monographs and Serials." *Journal of Library Administration* 12 (3): 41-49 (1990).

> Critical of the publishing industry, the authors' data show that a few publishers account for the bulk of cost increases suffered by libraries in recent years.

Hamilton, David P. "Trivia Pursuit." *The Washington Monthly* 23 (3): 36-42 (March 1991).

> The author contends that much scholarly publishing is not significant.

Hewitt, Joe A. "Altered States: Evolution or Revolution in Journal-Based Communications?" *American Libraries* 20:497-500 (1989).

> A critical look at the journal system of scholarly publishing and an indication that problems underlying scholarly publishing must and will be dealt with.

Holden, Constance. "Libraries Stunned by Journal Price Increases." *Science* 236:908-909 (Mar 22, 1987).

> Library problems due to escalating prices explained to scientific audiences.

Ivins, October, ed. "Do Serials Vendor Policies Affect Serials Pricing?" *Serials Review* 16 (2): 7-27 (Summer 1990).

> A dialogue among librarians, vendors, and publishers attempts to shed some light on the pricing issue.

Jeffrey, Nancy. "Mollusks, Semiotics and Dermatology: Narrow Scholarly Journals Are Spreading." *The Wall Street Journal*, August 27, 1987: 2:1.

> Criticism in the popular press of the minutia of some scholarly research and the costs of resulting publications.

"The Journal Pricing Issue: A Source List." *Library Issues* 8 (6): 1-4 (July 1988).

> A useful bibliography, carefully annotated, to early 1988.

Kingson, Jennifer A. "Where Information Is All, Pleas Arise for Less of It." *The New York Times*, 138 (47,926): E9 (Sunday, July 9, 1989).

> The popular press publicizes the glut of publications inundating libraries.

Lynden, Frederick C. "Cost Analysis of Monographs and Serials." *Journal of Library Administration* 12 (3): 19-39 (1990).

> Careful analysis of the pricing crisis with practical suggestions for collecting and using data and proposals for action on local and national levels.

Marks, Kenneth. "Longitudinal Study of Journal Prices in a Research Library." *The Serials Librarian* 19 (3/4): 105-135 (1991).

This study is remarkable for its breadth and basis of solid data. The authors' conclusions do not support some commonly held assumptions about serials price increases in recent years; very useful bibliographical references.

Mastejulia, Robert. "Publisher Policies and Their Impact on the Market." *Library Acquisitions: Practice & Theory* 11 (2): 139-144 (1987).

A vendor considers publisher behavior that affects book prices.

Milne, Dorothy, and Bill Tiffany. "A Survey of the Cost-Effectiveness of Serials: A Cost-Per-Use Method and Its Results." *The Serials Librarian* 19 (3/4): 137-150.

By calculating cost-per-use of certain serials, the authors demonstrate that a high percentage of serials are extremely costly on a per-use basis, a warning to publishers and an indication to librarians that other means of supply may be desirable.

Mitgang, Herbert. "American Libraries Are in Crisis Over the Cost of Scholarly Journals." *The New York Times* 148 (47,619): 11 (September 5, 1988).

Price increases of journals and resultant cancellation of subscriptions, along with comments by some prominent librarians, are explained for the general reader.

Mulvihill, Marguerite E. "Law Librarians Reconsider Rising Costs of Treatise Supplements." *Publishers Weekly* 237:34-35 (October 12, 1990).

Some librarians have responded to what they see as excessive and expensive loose-leaf law publishing by cancelling subscriptions and purchasing complete sets every two or three years.

Okerson, Ann, and Kendon Stubbs. "The Library 'Doomsday Machine.' " *Publishers Weekly* 238:36-37 (February 8, 1991).

An overview of the pricing crisis and a call for "a new paradigm for research libraries."

Webster, Duane E. "The Librarian's Response and Expectations." In *Issues for the New Decade: Today's Challenge, Tomorrow's Opportunity*, Alphonse F. Trezza, editor, 59-72. Boston, Mass.: G. K. Hall & Co., 1991.

Webster sees the solution to libraries' inability to purchase needed materials in "a new partnership between librarians and scholars."

RESOURCE SHARING

Ballard, Thomas H. "The Unfulfilled Promise of Resource Sharing." *American Libraries* 21:990-993 (Nov. 1990).

> Data show that while libraries pay lip service to resource sharing, interlibrary loan activity has increased far less than overall circulation in U.S. public libraries.

Sloan, Bernard G. *Linked Systems for Research Sharing*. Boston, Mass.: G.K. Hall & Co., 1990.

> An up-to-date, informative guide and theoretical framework for librarians working with linked systems for resource sharing; essential reading as such systems, their promises, and problems become more widespread.

RESOURCE SHARING: SERIALS

Cargill, Jennifer, and Diane J. Graves, eds. *Advances in Library Resource Sharing*. Westport, CT.: Meckler. Vol. 1- 1990- .

> Only one volume has been issued to date, but this serial promises to be an important vehicle for information about resource sharing among all types of libraries. Volume 1 includes an excellent, annotated bibliography.

Journal of Interlibrary Loan & Information Supply. Binghamton, N.Y.: Haworth Press. Vol. 1- .1990- .

> In addition to its emphasis on technological advances relating to resource sharing (see Ch. 1 bibliography), this periodical carries up-do-date articles on all aspects of interlending and document delivery; essential for keeping abreast of developments in this field.

CHAPTER 11: EVALUATION

Articles dealing with the evaluation of approval plan vendors will be found in the bibliography for Chapter 7: Approval Plans.

EVALUATION OF BOOK VENDORS

Alldredge, Noreen S. "The Preparation of Guidelines for Evaluating Performance of Vendors for In-Print Monographs." In *Issues in Acquisitions: Programs & Evaluation*, edited by Sul Lee, 1-10. Ann Arbor: Pierian Press, 1984.

> A member of the ALA subcommittee that developed the guidelines; presents valuable background information on their development and the need for regular, objective assessment of vendor performance; a good bibliography includes guides to placing orders and evaluating vendors.

American Library Association. Collection Management and Development Committee. *Guide to Performance Evaluation of Library Materials Vendors*. (Acquisitions Guidelines, no. 5). Chicago: American Library Association, 1988.

> Although it claims to be "only a beginning," this booklet is solid basis for the development of qualitative and quantitative measures of the performance of firm-order vendors.

Association for Higher Education of North Texas. Vendor Study Group. "Vendor Evaluation: A Selected Annotated Bibliography, 1955-1987." *Library Acquisitions: Practice & Theory* 12:17-28 (1988).

> This bibliography brings together significant articles relating to evaluation of book and serial vendors as well as publishers. Approval plan evaluations are excluded.

Barker, Joseph W. "Random Vendor Assignment in Vendor Performance Evaluation." *Library Acquisitions: Practice & Theory* 10 (4): 265-280 (1986).

> An excellent discussion of a relatively easy to manage but equitable vendor study designed to answer a number of questions about firm-order vendors. The methodology described here could be adapted for use by a great variety of libraries.

Davis, Mary Byrd. "Model for a Vendor Study in a Manual or Semi-Automated Acquisitions System." *Library Acquisitions: Practice & Theory* 3:53-60 (1979).

> A very useful article on firm-order vendor evaluation based on random sampling of orders; good discussion of underlying principles.

EVALUATING SERIALS VENDORS

Bonk, Sharon C. "Toward a Methodology of Evaluating Serials Vendors." *Library Acquisitions: Practice & Theory* 9 (1): 51-60 (1985).

> This is the most valuable guide to date on evaluating nonperiodical serials vendors; essential for anyone who buys serials.

STATISTICS

Carpenter, Ray L., and Ellen Storey Vacu. *Statistical Methods for Libraries*. Chicago, Ill.: American Library Association, 1978.

> Basic information on the whys and wherefores of basic research using statistical analysis for librarians.

Hartwig, Frederick. *Exploratory data analysis*. Quantitative applications in the social sciences, no. 16. Beverly Hills: Sage Publications, 1979.

Basic introduction to statistical analysis for the beginner.

Simpson, I.S. *Basic Statistics for Librarians*. Chicago, Ill.: American Library Association, 1988.

A useful guide for the statistically untrained librarian.

CHAPTER 12: A QUESTION OF ETHICS

ARTICLES

Bhide, Amar, and Howard H. Stevenson. "Why Be Honest if Honesty Doesn't Pay." *Harvard Business Review* 68 (5): 121-129 (Sept.-Oct. 1990).

A revealing examination of ethics in the world of business; perfectly applicable to librarians and their suppliers of materials.

Boissonnas, Christian M. "The Cost Is More Than that Elegant Dinner: Your Ethics Are at Steak." *Library Acquisitions: Practice & Theory* 11 (2): 145-152 (1987).

An acquisitions librarian takes a close look at some common practices and finds them wanting from an ethical point of view.

Dole, Wanda V. "Librarians, Publishers, and Vendors: Looking for Mr. Goodbuy." *Library Acquisitions: Practice & Theory* 11 (2): 125-34 (1987).

A clear look at the different and sometimes conflicting viewpoints of librarians, publishers, and vendors with suggestions for improving relations and adhering to ethical behavior.

Kanner, Bernice. "What Price Ethics? The Morality of the Eighties." *New York* 19 (27): 28-34 (July 14, 1986).

A discourse on the state of ethics in present-day American society.

BOOKS

Hauptman, Robert. *Ethical Challenges in Librarianship*. Phoenix, Ariz.: Oryx Press, 1988.

Hauptman, the most active investigator of ethical issues in librarianship, has little to say about acquisitions, but his work is always thought provoking.

Lancaster, F. W., ed. *Ethics and the Librarian*. Urbana-Champaign, University of Illinois Graduate School of Library and Information Service, 1991.

This current book includes much thought-provoking material, some of which is applicable to acquisitions work.

Lindsey, Jonathan A., and Ann E. Prentice. *Professional Ethics and Librarians*. Phoenix, Ariz.: Oryx Press, 1985.

This book contains a useful review of the historical development of and changes in codes of ethics for librarians. Careful reading will reveal minor references to acquisitions-related topics. The "Selected Bibliography" is of value.

Strauch, Katina, and Bruce Strauch, eds. *Legal and Ethical Issues in Acquisitions*. New York: Haworth Press, 1990.

No other book expressly links acquisitions and ethics. Although somewhat uneven, this book is essential to an understanding of current ethical questions relating to the purchase of library materials. Also published as *The Acquisitions Librarian* no. 3.

INDEX

AGRICOLA, 89
ARL *See* Association of Research Libraries
Abel, Richard, 5, 69
Acquisitions departments, 3
  automation, 51, 59-60
  evaluation of, 138-139
  role of, 3-4, 71
    in evaluation of vendors, 130-131
  University at Albany Libraries, 29, 42, 49, 72, 73, 85, 113, 114, 128, 133, 136, 143
Acquisitions librarians
  and ethics, 4, 141-142, 143-149
  professional activities and responsibilities, 4, 5, 9, 11, 24, 25, 28, 59, 62, 65-67, 91, 94-95, 117-120, 125
ADONIS project, 16
Agriculture Canada Library, 11
Alley, Brian, 147
American Library Association, 9, 25, 34, 59, 126, 131, 135, 141
  Annual Meeting, 26, 147
  Association for Library Collections & Technical Services, 141
    Serials Section Acquisitions Committee, 126
  code of ethics, 141, 148
  Professional Ethics Committee, 141
Amherst College, 121
Approval plans, 3, 7, 8, 9, 14, 20, 23, 25, 57
  automation of, 78-79
  development, 69
  discounts, 73
  evaluation of, 131-133
  function, 69-70
  future of, 79-81
  management, 70-73
  management reports, 74
  profiles, 74
  selection of, 75-76
  tape loading of bibliographic records, 72
Association of Research Libraries, 70, 110

B. Dalton, 13
BISAC *See* Book Industry Systems Advisory Committee
BITNET, 88
Baker & Taylor, 13, 96
  Approval Program, 79
Barker, Joe, 97, 100, 105, 137, 138
Berry, John, 140
Bhide, Amar, 149
Bids, 62-66
Blackwell, 16
Boissonnas, Christian, 118
Bonk, Sharon, 135
Book Industry Systems Advisory Committee, 12
Bookland EAN, 12
BookQuest, 104
Boyer, Calvin, 62

CARL System, 16
CD-ROM, 78, 83, 86-87, 89, 90, 91, 113, 119, 146
CPI *See* Consumer Price Index
Cancellations, 26, 37, 39, 56
Cargill, Jennifer S., 147
Center for Research Libraries, 64
Charleston Conference, 107, 117
Claims, 13, 32, 36, 37, 52, 54-55, 102, 103, 135, 142, 145, 146
Collection Development Policy, 4-5, 97, 103, 120-121, 123, 132
Communication
  value of, 55, 57, 58-59, 117, 123, 140, 145, 146, 150
CompuServe, 87, 88
Consumer Price Index, 113, 118
Continuations, 46-48, 134
Contracts, 61-62, 64-67
Cooperative collection development, 120-122
Cost-plus pricing, 21-23
Country of origin purchasing, 28, 36, 38, 46, 49

dBASE

II, 100
III, 100, 138
Dialog, 87, 88
Direct orders *See* Publishers as distributors
Discounts, 6, 8, 9, 21-23, 24, 31, 46, 47, 48, 102, 116, 130, 133, 142, 144, 146, 149
  librarians' demand for, 144
  See also Approval plans, discounts
Documents, *See* government publications
Dollar, U.S., 4, 46, 119
  loss of buying power, 71, 107, 113-114
  payment in, 46, 58

EBSCO Missing Issues Bank, 103
EC *See* European Community
EDI *See* electronic data interchange
Electronic data interchange, 12-15
Electronic publishing, 15, 16, 83-84, 87-88, 90
Elsevier, 16
Ethics, 141-150
European Community, 28, 117
Evaluation of vendors *See* Vendors, evaluation of

F.W. Faxon Company, 104
Farmington Plan, 69
Federal Deposit Insurance Corporation, 89
Federal Employee Identification Number, 33
Full text document delivery, 15-17, 97, 103, 119

GPO *See* Government Printing Office
German mark, 114
Government Printing Office, 88, 89
  Information Technology Program, 89

189

Government publications, 88-89

Hammaker, Charles, 118
Hampshire College, 121
Harvard University, 111
Harvard Medical School, 112
Hewitt, Joe, 9

ISBN, 12, 51, 90, 131, 139
ISI *See* Institute for Scientific Information
ISO *See* International Standards Organization
ISSN, 12, 38
Inflation, 36, 44, 69, 107, 113, 115
Information,
 proliferation of, 111-113
Ingram, 13, 96
Institute for Scientific Information, 112
Interlibrary loan, 15, 103, 121, 122
Internal Revenue Service, 89
International Standards Organization, 11
Internet, 88
Invoices, 13, 26, 40, 60
 tape loading of, 9, 37, 41-42, 51

Japanese yen, 114

Kruger, Betsy, 118
Kuntz, Harry, 34

Lexis, 87
Lindsey, Jonathan A., 141, 142
Lochman, Ed, 1

Mann, Peter, 107
Medis, 87
Melcher, Daniel, 63
Merriman, John, 32
Microforms, 47, 83, 84, 88, 90
Mt. Holyoke College, 121

NASA, 89
NIOSH, 89
NISO *See* National Information Standards Organization
NREN *See* National Research and Education Network
NTIS *See* National Technical Information Service
National Agricultural Library, 89
National Information Standards Organization, 12
National Institutes of Health, 89
National Research and Education Network, 17, 88, 120
National Technical Information Service, 88
Net pricing, 108-109
New York State Book Contract, 61
New York State Contract Reporter, 64
Nexis, 87
Nonprint media, 83-91
Nuzzo, David, 100

OCLC, 11, 52
OSH-ROM, 89
OSI *See* Open Systems Interchange
Open Systems Interchange, 11
Orders, 3, 6, 7, 19, 21, 29, 51-52
 firm, 108, 118, 125, 126, 129, 131, 133, 135, 137
 and approval plans, 71, 75, 77, 79
 and out-of-print orders, 97
 rush, 53, 127, 129, 131
 serial, 31-32, 37, 47, 51, 54
 verification of, 52
Out-Of-Print & Antiquarian Book Market Seminar, 95
Out-of-print books, 6, 95-96
 condition, 99

 ordering, 100-101
 prices of, 99
Out-of-print dealers, 94-95
 catalogs, 100
 relationships with libraries, 93-94, 101-103
Out-of-print orders *See* out-of-print books, ordering
Out-of-print serials
 online matching services, 104-105
 ordering, 103-104
Oxford University Press, 72

Partnership between vendors and librarians, 8-10, 11, 26, 28, 29, 31, 40, 46, 49, 51-60, 66-67, 76-78, 81, 89-91, 99, 102-103, 107, 118, 122-123, 135-136, 139-140, 149-150
Payment, 3, 8, 20, 24, 27, 33, 36, 37, 38, 40, 46, 57, 58, 63, 64, 72, 85, 98, 100, 102, 143, 146, 149
 See also Invoices; Prepayment plans
Pergamon, 16
Periodicals, 31-46
Prentice, Ann E., 141, 142
Prepayment plans, 37, 40-41, 116
Prices, 107-123
 of books, 21-23, 24, 28, 99
 of serials, 35-36, 44, 108-111
 See also Discounts; Service charge; Cost-plus pricing; Unbundling; Out-of-print books, prices of
Publishers, 40, 52-53
 as distributors, 20, 32, 33, 46-47
 role in price escalation, 108-110, 115
Pubnet, 13

RFP *See* Request for Proposal
RLIN, 52
Receiving, 3, 57, 71, 128

Reidelbach, John H., 75
Remainder dealers, 96
Reports, management, 6,7, 14, 33, 37, 41, 48, 60, 71, 74
Reports, status, 12, 14, 53
Request for Proposal, 66
Resource sharing, 121-122
Returns, 26, 55-56
of approval books, 71, 74, 75, 77

SALALM *See* Seminar on the Acquisition of Latin American Library Materials
SDI *See* Selective Dissemination of Information
SISAC *See* Serials Industry Systems Advisory Committee
Schmidt, Karen A., 76
Selection of suppliers *See* Vendors, selection of
Selective Dissemination of Information, 80
Seminar on the Acquisition of Latin American Library Materials, 25, 26
Serial orders *See* Orders, serial
Serial suppliers *See* Vendors, selection of
Serials Industry Systems Advisory Committee, 12

Serials, 31-49
SerialsQuest, 104
Service charge, 8, 22, 29, 35, 41, 43-45, 57, 65, 90, 127, 136, 143
Services *See* Vendors, services of
Shirk, Gary M., 75
Smith College, 121
Special Libraries Association, 25
Springer Verlag, 16
St. Clair, Gloriana, 118, 132, 138
State University of New York, 121
Stevenson, Howard H., 149
Subscription agents *See* Vendors

Technical standards, 11-12, 17, 27, 81, 87, 122
Texas A&M University, 138
Treadwell, Jane, 118, 132, 138

USBE *See* Universal Serials and Book Exchange
Unbundling, 45-46
United Nations, 13, 89
United States Geological Survey, 89
Universal Serials and Book Exchange, 103

University Microfilms, 90, 91
University of California, 121
University of California at Berkeley, 137
University of Illinois at Urbana-Champaign, 76
University of Massachusetts, 121

Vendors
and ethics, 142-143, 149-150
as distributors, 19-21, 116
evaluation of, 26-27, 28, 48, 57, 75, 125-140
foreign, 25-26, 27-29, 35-36, 46, 58, 69
identification of, 25-26, 34-35
role of, 5-8, 19-21, 32
selection of, 26-29, 34-35, 45-46, 48-49
services of, 23-24, 36-43

Waldenbooks, 13
Warzala, Martin, 79

X-12, 13-14, 59

Heather S. Miller is Head of the Acquisitions Department of the University at Albany Libraries, State University of New York.

Book design: Gloria Brown
Cover design: Apicella Design
Typography: C. Roberts